HOMESTYLE

cookies, muffins and cakes

MURDOCH BOOKS

contents

Heavenly home-made treats

There is nothing more satisfying than filling the biscuit tin with scrumptious home-baked cookies and muffins. Or serving your favourite home-made cake to appreciative friends or family, especially when they ask you for the recipe afterwards.

Novice bakers can be overwhelmed by the technical aspects of baking. Potentially, there's much that can go wrong—the baker's worst nightmare involves cakes that don't rise, biscuits that spread too thin and muffin mixtures oozing out of tins in the oven. But by observing a few simple rules that commonly apply to almost all types of baking, success can be assured. Firstly, it is vital to read a recipe thoroughly before starting, to check you have all the ingredients and the correct-sized tins at hand. Tins and trays should be greased or lined as specified, and the oven preheated, before doing anything. Make sure ingredients are at room temperature before starting—especially butter (unless, of course, a recipe states otherwise). Room-temperature eggs, butter, sugar and flour will amalgamate much easier than chilled ones—in fact when creaming butter with sugar (an essential step for many cakes and biscuits), the butter should be softened first. All ingredients must be measured and weighed accurately or all-important ratios (of liquid to dry ingredients, for example) will be upset. Consider buying a set of digital scales which, although expensive, last a very long time if looked after and offer by far the most accurate method of weighing. Similarly, measuring cups and a set of measuring spoons (which include a tablespoon, teaspoon and half teaspoon, among others) are indispensable.

There are literally hundreds of recipes for baked goods in circulation; these range from the highly complex and fiddly, to the downright homey and simple. More often than not, it is the latter that are most appreciated and it is these that star in this inspiring volume. Shortbread, gingerbread, brownies, biscotti, Madeira cake, banana muffins and classic sponge cake are all wonderfully uncomplicated yet their soothing familiarity never goes out of fashion or favour. Bought biscuits and cakes, while convenient, in no way compare to their home-made equivalents in either taste or texture. And some bought varieties are manufactured using unhealthy ingredients, such as trans fats, in order to lengthen the shelf-life and stabilise flavours. For this and many other good reasons, once you start baking yourself, there is no going back to store-bought.

Cookies

Vanilla custard kisses

PREPARATION TIME: 15 MINUTES I TOTAL COOKING TIME: 12 MINUTES I MAKES 26

125 g (4½ oz) unsalted butter
125 g (4½ oz/½ cup) caster (superfine) sugar
2 egg yolks, lightly beaten
2 teaspoons vanilla essence
60 g (2¼ oz/½ cup) custard powder
250 g (9 oz/2 cups) plain (all-purpose) flour

VANILLA CREAM
40 g (1½ oz) unsalted butter, softened
1 teaspoon vanilla essence
90 g (3¼ oz/¾ cup) icing (confectioners')
    sugar
1 tablespoon milk

1   Preheat the oven to 180°C (350°F/Gas 4). Grease two baking trays and line each with baking paper. Using electric beaters, beat the butter and sugar in a small mixing bowl until the mixture is light and creamy. Add the egg yolks gradually, beating the mixture thoroughly after each addition. Add the vanilla essence and beat until combined.

2   Transfer the mixture to a large mixing bowl. Using a metal spoon, fold in the sifted custard powder and flour. Stir until the ingredients are just combined and the mixture is almost smooth. Press the mixture together with fingertips to form a soft dough.

3   Roll 1 level teaspoon of mixture at a time into balls. Arrange about 5 cm (2 inches) apart on the prepared trays. Flatten lightly with the base of a glass into 2.5 cm (1 inch) rounds. Bake for 12 minutes, or until golden.

4   To make the vanilla cream, beat the butter and vanilla in a small bowl with a wooden spoon until smooth. Add the sifted icing sugar and milk gradually, stirring until the mixture is smooth. Leave the biscuits on the trays for 5 minutes then transfer to a wire rack to cool. Spread half the biscuits with vanilla cream and sandwich together with the remaining biscuits.

STORAGE: *Store the biscuits in an airtight container for up to 2 days.*

Beat the butter and sugar until light and creamy, then gradually add the egg yolks to the mixture.

Gently fold the sifted custard powder and flour into the mixture with a metal spoon.

Roll the mixture into balls and place on a prepared baking tray before slightly flattening.

Cinnamon pecan biscuits

PREPARATION TIME: 20 MINUTES | TOTAL COOKING TIME: 15 MINUTES | MAKES 50

100 g (3½ oz) dark chocolate
125 g (4½ oz) unsalted butter
125 g (4½ oz/½ cup) caster (superfine) sugar
1 egg, lightly beaten
75 g (2½ oz) finely chopped pecans
200 g (7 oz/1⅔ cups) plain (all-purpose) flour
2 teaspoons ground cinnamon
    (see VARIATION)
100 g (3½ oz/1 cup) whole pecans, for
    decoration (see HINT)
1 tablespoon icing (confectioners') sugar,
    to dust

1 Preheat the oven to 180°C (350°F/Gas 4).
Line two baking trays with baking paper.
Chop the chocolate and place in a small
heatproof bowl. Stand over a pan of simmering
water. Stir until the chocolate is melted and
smooth. Allow to cool but not to reset.

2 Using electric beaters, beat the butter
and sugar in a small mixing bowl until light
and creamy. Add the egg gradually, beating
thoroughly. Add the cooled melted chocolate
and beat until combined.

3 Transfer mixture to a large bowl and add the
chopped pecans. Using a metal spoon, fold in the
sifted flour and cinnamon. Stir until ingredients
are combined but do not overbeat. Lightly roll
2 teaspoons of the mixture into oval shapes with
floured hands, place on the prepared trays and
press a pecan onto each. Bake for 10 minutes, or
until lightly browned.

4 Transfer to a wire rack to cool completely.
Lightly dust each biscuit with the icing sugar.

STORAGE: *Store for up to 2 days in an airtight
container in a cool, dark place.*

VARIATION: *Use mixed (pumpkin pie) spice
or allspice in place of the cinnamon.*

HINT: *If preferred, bake the biscuits without
the pecan on top. When baked and cooled, dip
the top of each biscuit in melted chocolate and
press a pecan on top.*

Stand a small heatproof bowl over a pan of
simmering water and melt the chocolate.

Roll the mixture into oval shapes, place on the
prepared tray and press pecans on top.

Chocolate fudge brownies

PREPARATION TIME: 15 MINUTES + 1 HOUR REFRIGERATION | TOTAL COOKING TIME: 12 MINUTES | MAKES 30

150 g (5½ oz/1¼ cups) plain (all-purpose) flour
125 g (4½ oz/1 cup) chopped walnuts
90 g (3¼ oz/½ cup) chocolate chips
125 g (4½ oz) unsalted butter, chopped
200 g (7 oz) dark chocolate, chopped
2 tablespoons golden syrup (if unavailable, substitute with half honey and half dark corn syrup)
2 eggs, lightly beaten

1 Line two baking trays with baking paper. Sift the flour into a large mixing bowl. Add the walnuts and chocolate chips and make a well in the centre.

2 Combine the butter and dark chocolate in a small saucepan. Stir over low heat for 5 minutes, or until the chocolate has melted and the mixture is smooth. Remove the pan from the heat, add the syrup and beaten eggs, mixing well.

3 Pour the chocolate mixture into a large mixing bowl with the dry ingredients. Using a metal spoon, stir until just combined. Cover with plastic wrap and refrigerate for 1 hour.

4 Preheat the oven to 180°C (350°F/Gas 4). Roll 1 level tablespoon of mixture at a time into a ball. Arrange the balls on the prepared trays and bake for 12 minutes. (The biscuits will still be soft at this stage, but they will become firm on standing.) Remove the biscuits from the oven and transfer to a wire rack to cool completely.

STORAGE: *The brownies may be stored in an airtight container for up to 2 days.*

NOTE: *These rich, chocolate brownies have a delicious fudge-like texture. Sprinkle brownies with chocolate sprinkles before baking, if desired. This brownie mixture can also be baked in a tin as a slice and cut into fingers when cooked. Spread with your favourite rich chocolate icing before cutting, if desired.*

Stir the chocolate mixture into the dry ingredients until they are just combined.

Roll the mixture into balls and place on the prepared trays, allowing a little room for spreading.

Shortbread stars with lemon glaze

PREPARATION TIME: 20 MINUTES | TOTAL COOKING TIME: 15 MINUTES | MAKES 35

310 g (11 oz/2½ cups) plain (all-purpose) flour
2 tablespoons rice flour
200 g (7 oz) unsalted butter
40 g (1½ oz/⅓ cup) icing (confectioners') sugar
1 teaspoon finely grated lemon zest
2 tablespoons lemon juice
silver cachous, to decorate

LEMON GLAZE
125 g (4½ oz/1 cup) icing (confectioners') sugar
2 tablespoons lemon juice, strained
yellow or orange food colouring

1 Preheat the oven to 180°C (350°F/Gas 4). Line two baking trays with baking paper. Place the flours, butter and icing sugar in a food processor and process for 30 seconds or until the mixture is fine and crumbly. Add the lemon zest and juice and process for 20 seconds or until the mixture forms a soft dough.

2 Turn out onto a lightly floured surface and knead for 20 seconds or until smooth. Roll the dough out to 7 mm (⅜ inch) thickness. Using a 6 cm (2½ inch) star cutter, cut out shapes. Bake for 15 minutes or until golden. Transfer to a wire rack to cool.

3 To make the lemon glaze, place the icing sugar and lemon juice in a heatproof bowl over a saucepan of hot water. Stir until smooth. Dip the biscuits face down in the glaze and drain any excess. Dip a fine paintbrush or skewer into food colouring and draw lines on the icing before it sets. Decorate with a cachou.

STORAGE: *Store for up to 5 days in an airtight container in a cool, dark place.*

Add the lemon zest and lemon juice to the mixture in the food processor.

Use a 6 cm (2½ inch) cookie cutter to cut the star shapes out of the dough.

Use a skewer to carefully draw coloured lines into the icing before it sets.

Jam drops

PREPARATION TIME: 20 MINUTES | TOTAL COOKING TIME: 10–12 MINUTES | MAKES 26

80 g (2¾ oz) unsalted butter, softened
90 g (3¼ oz/⅓ cup) caster (superfine) sugar
2 tablespoons milk
½ teaspoon vanilla essence
175 g (6 oz/1½ cups) plain (all-purpose) flour
40 g (1½ oz/⅓ cup) custard powder
105 g (3½ oz/⅓ cup) raspberry jam

1 Preheat the oven to 180°C (350°F/Gas 4). Line two baking trays with baking paper.

2 Cream the butter and sugar in a mixing bowl with electric beaters until light and fluffy. Add the milk and vanilla and beat until well combined. Add the sifted flour and custard powder and mix with a flat-bladed knife to form a soft dough. Roll heaped teaspoons of the mixture into balls and place on the prepared trays.

3 Make an indentation in each ball using the end of a wooden spoon. Fill each hole with a little jam.

4 Bake for 10–12 minutes, or until lightly golden. Cool slightly on the trays, then transfer to a wire rack to cool completely.

STORAGE: *These will keep for up to 3 days in an airtight container.*

Beat the softened butter and sugar together until they are pale and fluffy.

Use a flat-bladed knife to mix the ingredients with a cutting, rather than a stirring, motion.

Fill the centre of each ball with raspberry jam. Apricot jam can also be used.

Monte creams

PREPARATION TIME: 30 MINUTES I TOTAL COOKING TIME: 20 MINUTES I MAKES 13

125 g (4½ oz) unsalted butter
125 g (4½ oz/½ cup) caster (superfine) sugar
3 tablespoons milk
220 g (7¾ oz/1¾ cups) plain (all-purpose) flour
30 g (1 oz/¼ cup) custard powder
30 g (1 oz/⅓ cup) desiccated coconut

FILLING
75 g (2½ oz) unsalted butter, softened
90 g (3¼ oz/¾ cup) icing (confectioners') sugar
2 teaspoons milk
105 g (3½ oz/⅓ cup) strawberry jam

1   Preheat the oven to 180°C (350°F/Gas 4). Line two baking trays with baking paper.

2   Using electric beaters, cream the butter and sugar in a small mixing bowl until light and fluffy. Add the milk and beat until combined. Sift the flour and custard powder together and add to the bowl with the coconut. Mix to form a soft dough.

3   Roll the mixture into balls using 1 heaped teaspoon at a time. Place on the prepared trays, making sure they are spaced enough to allow for spreading during baking, and press with a fork. Dip the fork in custard powder occasionally to prevent it from sticking. Bake for 15–20 minutes, or until just golden. Transfer the biscuits to a wire rack to cool completely before filling.

4   For the filling, beat the butter and icing sugar in a small bowl with electric beaters until light and creamy. Beat in the milk. Spread one biscuit with ½ teaspoon of the filling and one with ½ teaspoon of jam, then press them together.

STORAGE: *These will keep for up to 4 days in an airtight container.*

Roll the dough into balls, place on the prepared trays and press firmly with a fork.

Sandwich the cooled biscuits together with the jam and butter mixture.

Lebkuchen

PREPARATION TIME: 25 MINUTES | TOTAL COOKING TIME: 30 MINUTES | MAKES 40

350 g (12 oz/2¾ cups) plain (all-purpose) flour

60 g (2¼ oz/½ cup) cornflour (cornstarch)

2 teaspoons unsweetened cocoa powder

1 teaspoon mixed (pumpkin pie) spice

1 teaspoon ground cinnamon

½ teaspoon ground nutmeg

100 g (3½ oz) unsalted butter, cubed

260 g (9¼ oz/¾ cup) golden syrup (if unavailable, substitute with half honey and half dark corn syrup)

2 tablespoons milk

150 g (5½ oz/1 cup) white chocolate melts (buttons)

¼ teaspoon mixed (pumpkin pie) spice, extra, to sprinkle

1 Preheat the oven to 180°C (350°F/Gas 4). Line two baking trays with baking paper.

2 Sift the plain flour and cornflour, cocoa and spices into a large bowl and make a well in the centre.

3 Place the butter, golden syrup and milk in a small saucepan, and stir over low heat until the butter has melted and the mixture is smooth. Remove from the heat and add to the dry ingredients. Mix with a flat-bladed knife until ingredients come together in small beads. Gather together with your hands and turn out onto a sheet of baking paper.

4 Roll the dough out to about 7 mm (⅜ inch) thick. Cut into heart shapes using a 6 cm (2½ inch) cookie cutter. Place on the prepared trays and bake for 20 minutes, or until lightly browned. Cool slightly, then transfer to a wire rack until the biscuits are completely cool.

5 Place the chocolate in a heatproof bowl. Bring a saucepan of water to the boil, then remove from heat. Sit the bowl over the pan, making sure the base does not touch the water. Stir until the chocolate has melted.

6 Dip one half of each biscuit into the chocolate and place on a sheet of baking paper until set. Sprinkle with mixed spice.

STORAGE: *These biscuits can be stored in an airtight container for up to 5 days.*

Carefully transfer the dough shapes to the prepared baking tray using a flat-bladed knife.

Dip one half of each biscuit into the melted chocolate and place on a sheet of baking paper.

Chocolate butter fingers

PREPARATION TIME: 30 MINUTES | TOTAL COOKING TIME: 15 MINUTES | MAKES 40

125 g (4½ oz) unsalted butter
40 g (1½ oz/⅓ cup) icing (confectioners') sugar
½ teaspoon vanilla essence
½ teaspoon grated lemon zest
1 teaspoon cream
60 g (2¼ oz/½ cup) cornflour (cornstarch)
80 g (2¾ oz/⅔ cup) plain (all-purpose) flour
60 g (2¼ oz) chocolate melts (buttons), melted

1 Preheat the oven to 180°C (350°F/Gas 4). Lightly grease two baking trays and line with baking paper. Using electric beaters, beat the butter and sugar until light and creamy. Add the vanilla, lemon zest and cream, and beat until combined. Add the sifted flours and beat until the mixture is smooth enough for piping.

2 Spoon the mixture into a piping (icing) bag fitted with a 1.5 cm (⅝ inch) star nozzle. Pipe 4 cm (1½ inch) lengths onto the prepared trays. Bake the biscuits for 15 minutes, or until lightly golden. Cool the biscuits on the trays before transferring to a wire rack.

3 Place the melted chocolate into a small paper piping (icing) bag and snip off the tip. Drizzle diagonally over the fingers. Allow to set. Serve.

STORAGE: *These biscuits can be made up to 3 days in advance. Store in an airtight container in a cool, dark place.*

NOTE: *Decorate with dark or white chocolate, or dust with combined icing sugar and cocoa. When melting the chocolate, take care not to let water come into contact with the melting mixture or it will begin to seize and start to harden immediately.*

Pipe lengths of the mixture onto the prepared trays and place in the oven for baking.

Drizzle the melted chocolate across the biscuits in a zigzag pattern and leave to set.

Two-tone biscuits

PREPARATION TIME: 30 MINUTES + 20 MINUTES REFRIGERATION | TOTAL COOKING TIME: 10–12 MINUTES | MAKES ABOUT 25

125 g (4½ oz) unsalted butter
90 g (3¼ oz/¾ cup) icing (confectioners') sugar
1 egg
200 g (7 oz/1⅔ cups) plain (all-purpose) flour
1 tablespoon cornflour (cornstarch)
2 tablespoons unsweetened cocoa powder
50 g (1¾ oz) dark cooking chocolate, melted

1 Preheat the oven to 180°C (350°F/Gas 4). Line two baking trays with baking paper. Using electric beaters, beat the butter and icing sugar in a large mixing bowl until light and creamy. Add the egg and beat until smooth. Add the sifted plain flour and cornflour and mix with a flat-bladed knife until well combined.

2 Divide the mixture evenly between two bowls. Only add the cocoa powder and melted chocolate to one portion, then mix both until well combined. Wrap the dough portions separately in plastic wrap and refrigerate for 20 minutes, or until firm.

3 Roll the dough portions separately between sheets of baking paper until 5 mm (¼ inch) thick. Use two sizes of cookie cutter of the same shape. Cut large shapes from each sheet of dough, then take the smaller cutter and cut a shape from inside the larger dough shape; swap inner shapes and assemble to make two-tone biscuits. Place on the prepared trays and bake for 10–12 minutes, or until just golden. Cool on the tray.

STORAGE: *These biscuits may be stored in an airtight container for up to 4 days.*

Place the butter and icing sugar in a large mixing bowl and beat until the mixture is light and creamy.

Add the cocoa and melted chocolate to half the mixture and mix with a flat-bladed knife.

Assemble the biscuits by placing smaller shapes inside bigger pieces of a different colour.

Viennese fingers

PREPARATION TIME: 20 MINUTES | TOTAL COOKING TIME: 12 MINUTES | MAKES 20

100 g (3½ oz) unsalted butter, softened
40 g (1½ oz/⅓ cup) icing (confectioners')
   sugar
2 egg yolks
1½ teaspoons vanilla essence
125 g (4½ oz/1 cup) plain (all-purpose) flour
100 g (3½ oz) dark cooking chocolate,
   chopped
30 g (1 oz) unsalted butter, extra, for icing

1 Preheat the oven to 180°C (350°F/Gas 4). Line two baking trays with baking paper.

2 Using electric beaters, cream the butter and icing sugar in a small mixing bowl until light and fluffy. Gradually add the egg yolks and vanilla and beat thoroughly. Transfer the mixture to a large mixing bowl, then sift in the flour. Using a flat-bladed knife, mix until just combined and the mixture is smooth.

3 Spoon the mixture into a piping (icing) bag fitted with a fluted 1 cm (½ inch) piping nozzle and pipe the mixture into wavy 6 cm (2½ inch) lengths on the prepared trays.

4 Bake the biscuits for 12 minutes, or until golden brown. Allow to cool slightly on the trays, then transfer to a wire rack to cool.

5 Place the chocolate and extra butter in a small heatproof bowl. Half-fill a saucepan with water and bring to the boil, then remove from the heat. Sit the bowl over the pan, making sure the base of the bowl does not sit in the water. Stir occasionally until the chocolate and butter have melted and the mixture is smooth. Dip half of each biscuit into the melted chocolate mixture and leave to set on baking paper or foil.

STORAGE: *Store in an airtight container for up to 2 days.*

NOTE: *To make piping easier, fold down the bag by 5 cm (2 inches) before adding the mixture, then unfold. The top will be clean and easy to twist, stopping any mixture from squirting out the top.*

Carefully pipe the biscuit mixture directly onto the prepared tray.

Dip the biscuits into the chocolate and butter mixture before leaving them to set.

Gingernuts

PREPARATION TIME: 25 MINUTES | TOTAL COOKING TIME: 15 MINUTES | MAKES 30

250 g (9 oz/2 cups) plain (all-purpose) flour
½ teaspoon bicarbonate of soda (baking soda)
1 tablespoon ground ginger
½ teaspoon mixed (pumpkin pie) spice
125 g (4½ oz) unsalted butter, chopped
185 g (6½ oz/1 cup) lightly packed soft brown
    sugar
60 ml (2 fl oz/¼ cup) boiling water
1 tablespoon golden syrup (if unavailable,
    substitute with half honey and half dark
    corn syrup)

1   Preheat the oven to 180°C (350°F/Gas 4). Line
two baking trays with baking paper.

2   Sift the flour, bicarbonate of soda, ginger
and mixed spice into a large mixing bowl. Add
the butter and sugar and rub into the flour with
your fingertips until the mixture resembles fine
breadcrumbs.

3   Pour the boiling water into a small heatproof
bowl, add the golden syrup and stir until
dissolved. Add to the flour mixture and mix to
a soft dough with a flat-bladed knife.

4   Roll into balls using 2 heaped teaspoons
of mixture at a time. Place on the prepared
trays, allowing enough room for spreading, and
flatten out slightly with your fingertips. Bake
for 15 minutes, or until well-coloured and firm.
Leave to cool on the trays for 10 minutes before
transferring to a wire rack to cool completely.
Repeat with the remaining mixture.

STORAGE: *Store in an airtight container for up
to 5 days.*

VARIATION: *If you want to dress the biscuits
up, make icing by combining 2–3 teaspoons
lemon juice, 60 g (2¼ oz/½ cup) sifted icing
(confectioners') sugar and 10 g (¼ oz) melted
butter in a small bowl. Mix until smooth, then
spread over the biscuits and allow to set.*

For a smooth mixture, sift the flour, bicarbonate of
soda, ginger and mixed spice.

Place the balls of dough on the prepared trays and
press with your fingertips to flatten.

Peanut butter cookies

PREPARATION TIME: 25 MINUTES I TOTAL COOKING TIME: 10 MINUTES I MAKES ABOUT 40

185 g (6½ oz/1½ cups) plain (all-purpose) flour
75 g (2½ oz/½ cup) self-raising flour
90 g (3¼ oz/1 cup) rolled (porridge) oats
125 g (4½ oz) unsalted butter
110 g (3¾ oz/½ cup) caster (superfine) sugar
120 g (4¼ oz/⅓ cup) honey
2 tablespoons peanut butter

TOPPING
120 g (4¼ oz/¾ cup) icing (confectioners')
    sugar
25 g (1 oz) unsalted butter, softened
1 tablespoon warm water
150 g (5½ oz/1 cup) roasted unsalted peanuts,
    finely chopped

1   Preheat the oven to 180°C (350°F/Gas 4).
Grease two baking trays. Sift the flours into a
large mixing bowl and stir in the oats.

2   Combine the butter, sugar, honey and peanut
butter in a saucepan and stir over medium heat
until melted. Add to the flour mixture. Using a
metal spoon, stir to just combine the ingredients.
Roll heaped teaspoons of mixture into balls.
Arrange on the prepared trays and press lightly
to flatten. Bake for 10 minutes, or until golden.
Cool the cookies on the trays.

3   To make the topping, combine the icing
sugar, butter and water in a small bowl. Stir until
smooth. Dip the tops of the cookies into the
topping, then into the nuts.

STORAGE: *Store for up to 4 days in an airtight*
container in a cool, dark place.

Pour the combined butter, sugar, honey and peanut butter into the flour and oat mixture.

Coat one side of the cookie with topping and then dip into the chopped nuts.

Gingerbread people

PREPARATION TIME: 40 MINUTES + 15 MINUTES REFRIGERATION | TOTAL COOKING TIME: 10 MINUTES | MAKES 8

125 g (4½ oz) unsalted butter, softened
60 g (2¼ oz/⅓ cup) lightly packed soft brown
    sugar
90 g (3¼ oz/¼ cup) golden syrup (if
    unavailable, substitute with half honey
    and half dark corn syrup)
1 egg, lightly beaten
300 g (10½ oz/2½ cups) plain (all-purpose)
    flour
1 tablespoon ground ginger
1 teaspoon bicarbonate of soda (baking soda)
1 tablespoon currants

ICING
1 egg white
½ teaspoon lemon juice
155 g (5½ oz/1¼ cups) icing (confectioners')
    sugar, sifted
assorted food colourings

1   Preheat the oven to 180°C (350°F/Gas 4). Line two baking trays with baking paper.

2   Using electric beaters, cream the butter, sugar and golden syrup in a large mixing bowl until light and fluffy. Add the egg gradually, beating well after each addition. Sift the dry ingredients over the butter mixture and mix with a flat-bladed knife until just combined. Combine the dough with your hands. Turn onto a well-floured surface and knead for 1–2 minutes, or until smooth. Roll out on a board, between two sheets of baking paper, to 5 mm (¼ inch) thick. Refrigerate on the board for 15 minutes to firm.

3   Cut the dough into shapes with a 13 cm (5 inch) gingerbread person cutter. Press the remaining dough together and re-roll. Cut out shapes and place the biscuits on the trays. Place the currants as eyes and noses. Bake for 10 minutes, or until lightly browned. Cool on the trays.

4   To make the icing (frosting), beat the egg white with electric beaters in a small, clean, dry bowl until foamy. Gradually add the lemon juice and icing sugar and beat until thick. Divide the icing among several bowls and add the food colourings. Spoon into small paper piping (icing) bags. Seal ends, snip the tips off the bags and pipe on faces and clothing.

STORAGE: *These biscuits can be stored in an airtight container for up to 3 days.*

Mix in the dry ingredients with a flat-bladed knife, using a cutting action.

Use a cookie cutter to cut out the gingerbread person shape.

Snip the tip off the piping (icing) bag to decorate the gingerbread people.

Choc-dipped macaroons

PREPARATION TIME: 25 MINUTES I TOTAL COOKING TIME: 15–18 MINUTES I MAKES ABOUT 32

1 egg white
90 g (3¼ oz/⅓ cup) caster (superfine) sugar
2 teaspoons cornflour (cornstarch)
90 g (3¼ oz/1 cup) desiccated coconut
65 g (2¼ oz) dark cooking chocolate

1   Preheat the oven to 160°C (315°F/ Gas 2–3). Line two baking trays with baking paper. Place the egg white in a small, dry bowl. Using electric beaters, beat until firm peaks form. Add the sugar gradually, beating constantly until the mixture is thick and glossy and all the sugar has dissolved. Add the cornflour and beat until the ingredients are just combined.

2   Add the coconut to the egg white mixture. Using a metal spoon, stir until just combined. Roll heaped teaspoons of the mixture into balls and place on the prepared trays. Bake for 15–18 minutes, or until the macaroons are lightly golden. Remove from the oven and leave to cool on the tray.

3   Place the chocolate in a small bowl over a pan of barely simmering water. When the chocolate is beginning to soften, stir until smooth. Dip the macaroons into the chocolate and allow the excess to drain. Place on a foil-lined tray and leave to set. Dust with cocoa powder if desired.

STORAGE: *Store the macaroons in an airtight container for 1 day.*

HINT: *These are delicious served with a soft, creamy dessert.*

Roll the macaroon mixture into balls and place on the prepared trays.

Dip the cooled macaroons into melted chocolate and leave to set.

Frosted crescents

PREPARATION TIME: 30 MINUTES | TOTAL COOKING TIME: 12 MINUTES | MAKES 45

60 g (2¼ oz) roasted macadamia nuts or almonds
125 g (4½ oz/1 cup) plain (all-purpose) flour
60 g (2¼ oz/¼ cup) sugar
½ teaspoon grated orange zest
   (see VARIATION)
125 g (4½ oz) unsalted butter, chopped
1 egg yolk
icing (confectioners') sugar, to dust

1 Preheat the oven to 170°C (325°F/Gas 3). Lightly grease two baking trays or line them with baking paper. Place the macadamia nuts or almonds in a food processor and process until finely crushed. Sift the flour into a medium bowl and add the sugar, orange zest and butter. Using your fingertips, rub the butter into the flour mixture for 5 minutes, or until the mixture is fine and crumbly. Add the egg yolk and ground nuts. Mix until well combined and the mixture forms a soft dough.

2 Shape level teaspoonfuls of the dough into small crescents and place on the prepared trays. Bake for 12 minutes or until pale golden in colour.

3 While the crescents are still warm, sift a generous amount of icing sugar over them. Stand the crescents for 2 minutes. Transfer to wire racks to cool completely.

STORAGE: *Make the crescents 1 week in advance. Store in an airtight container in a cool, dry place.*

VARIATION: *Use lemon zest instead of the orange zest, if desired. Add ¼ teaspoonful of orange-flower water to the dough for extra flavour.*

Rub the butter into the flour mixture then add the egg yolk and ground nuts.

Shape the dough into crescent shapes and place on the prepared trays.

Dust the crescent-shaped biscuits with icing sugar while they are still warm.

Hazelnut coffee biscuits

PREPARATION TIME: 1 HOUR + 20 MINUTES REFRIGERATION | TOTAL COOKING TIME: 25–35 MINUTES | MAKES 60

125 g (4½ oz) unsalted butter
125 g (4½ oz/½ cup) caster (superfine) sugar
1 teaspoon grated lemon zest
1 egg yolk
1 teaspoon lemon juice
125 g (4½ oz/1 cup) hazelnuts, ground
155 g (5½ oz/1¼ cups) plain (all-purpose) flour

ICING
125 g (4½ oz/1 cup) icing (confectioners') sugar, sifted
30 g (1 oz) unsalted butter, melted
3–4 teaspoons lemon juice

COFFEE CREAM
125 g (4½ oz/½ cup) caster (superfine) sugar
water
1 tablespoon instant coffee
80 g (2¾ oz) unsalted butter

1 Preheat the oven to 180°C (350°F/Gas 4). Line two baking trays with baking paper. Using electric beaters, beat the butter and sugar in a mixing bowl until light and creamy. Add the zest, egg yolk, juice and nuts. Beat until well combined. Using a metal spoon, stir in the sifted flour. Shape the dough into a smooth ball and cover in plastic wrap. Refrigerate for 20 minutes.

2 Divide the mixture in half. Roll one portion between two sheets of baking paper until 5 mm (¼ inch) thick. Using a 3 cm (1¼ inch) fluted cutter, cut out rounds and place on the prepared trays. Repeat with remaining dough. Bake for 10 minutes, or until biscuits are golden. Remove from oven and transfer to wire racks to cool.

3 To make the icing, combine the icing sugar and butter. Add enough lemon juice to form a smooth mixture. Place into a paper piping (icing) bag, snip off tip, and pipe icing onto each biscuit.

4 To make the coffee cream, combine the sugar, 60 ml (2 fl oz/¼ cup) water and coffee in a pan. Stir over low heat, without boiling, until the sugar dissolves. Bring to the boil, reduce heat and simmer, uncovered, without stirring for 4–5 minutes. Beat butter until light and creamy. Pour the cooled syrup in a thin stream, beating constantly until thick and glossy.

5 Place into a paper piping (icing) bag, snip off tip to an inverted 'V'. Pipe small rosettes on top of the iced biscuits.

STORAGE: *Make up to a week in advance but ice just before serving.*

Cut out the biscuits using a small fluted or smooth-edged cutter.

Add the cooled syrup to the beaten butter, beating constantly until thick and glossy.

Pipe icing onto each biscuit and top with a small rosette of coffee cream.

Amaretti

PREPARATION TIME: 15 MINUTES + 1 HOUR STANDING | TOTAL COOKING TIME: 20 MINUTES | MAKES 30

1 tablespoon plain (all-purpose) flour
1 tablespoon cornflour (cornstarch)
1 teaspoon ground cinnamon
160 g (5½ oz/⅔ cup) caster (superfine) sugar
95 g (3¼ oz/1 cup) ground almonds
1 teaspoon grated lemon zest
2 egg whites
30 g (1 oz/¼ cup) icing (confectioners') sugar

1   Line two baking trays with baking paper. Sift the flour, cornflour, cinnamon and half the caster sugar into a large bowl, then add the ground almonds and lemon zest.

2   Beat the egg whites in a clean, dry bowl with electric beaters until firm peaks form. Gradually add the remaining caster sugar, beating constantly until the mixture is thick and glossy and all the sugar has dissolved. Using a metal spoon, fold the egg white mixture into the dry ingredients and stir until the ingredients are just combined.

3   Roll 2 level teaspoons of mixture at a time with oiled or wetted hands into balls and arrange on the trays, allowing room for spreading. Set the trays aside, uncovered, for 1 hour.

4   Preheat the oven to 180°C (350°F/Gas 4). Sift the icing sugar liberally over the uncooked biscuits, then bake for 15–20 minutes, or until crisp and lightly browned. Transfer to a wire rack and leave to cool completely.

STORAGE: *These biscuits can be stored in an airtight container for up to 2 days.*

Using a metal spoon, gently fold the egg white mixture into the dry ingredients.

Oil or wet your hands to stop the mixture from sticking and then roll into balls.

Mixed nut biscotti

PREPARATION TIME: 30 MINUTES | TOTAL COOKING TIME: 45 MINUTES | MAKES ABOUT 50

25 g (1 oz) almonds (see VARIATION)
25 g (1 oz) hazelnuts
75 g (2½ oz) unsalted pistachios
3 egg whites
125 g (4½ oz/½ cup) caster (superfine) sugar
100 g (3½ oz/¾ cup) plain (all-purpose) flour

1 Preheat the oven to 180°C (350°F/Gas 4). Lightly grease a 26 x 8 x 4.5 cm (10½ x 3¼ x 1¾ inch) loaf (bar) tin and line the base and sides with baking paper. Spread the almonds, hazelnuts and pistachios onto a flat baking tray and place in the oven for 2–3 minutes, until the nuts are just toasted. Leave to cool. Place the egg whites in a small, clean, dry bowl. Using electric beaters, beat the egg whites until stiff peaks form. Add the sugar gradually, beating constantly until the mixture is thick and glossy and all the sugar has dissolved.

2 Transfer the mixture to a large mixing bowl. Add the sifted flour and nuts. Using a metal spoon, gently fold the ingredients together until well combined. Spread into the prepared tin and smooth the surface with a spoon. Bake for 25 minutes, or until set. Leave to cool completely in the tin.

3 Preheat the oven to 160°C (315°F/Gas 2–3). Using a sharp, serrated knife, cut the baked loaf into 5 mm (¼ inch) slices. Spread the slices onto prepared baking trays and bake for about 15 minutes, turning once halfway through cooking, until slices are lightly golden and crisp.

STORAGE: *The biscotti will keep for up to a week in an airtight container.*

VARIATION: *Use any combination of nuts, or a single variety, to the weight of 125 g (4½ oz).*

Using a metal spoon, fold the flour and nuts through the beaten egg whites.

Slice the biscotti loaf and bake for 15 minutes, or until lightly golden and crisp.

Triple chocolate peanut butter cookies

PREPARATION TIME: 30 MINUTES I TOTAL COOKING TIME: 30 MINUTES I MAKES ABOUT 34

125 g (4½ oz) unsalted butter

140 g (5 oz/¾ cup) lightly packed soft brown sugar

1 egg, lightly beaten

185 g (6½ oz/¾ cup) peanut butter (see HINTS)

165 g (5¾ oz/1⅓ cup) plain (all-purpose) flour, sifted

½ teaspoon bicarbonate of soda (baking soda)

25 g (1 oz/¼ cup) unsweetened cocoa powder

175 g (6 oz) white chocolate melts (buttons)

175 g (6 oz) dark chocolate melts (buttons)

1   Preheat the oven to 180°C (350°F/Gas 4). Line two baking trays with baking paper. Using electric beaters, beat the butter and sugar in a mixing bowl until light and creamy. Add the egg a little at a time, beating thoroughly after each addition. Add the peanut butter and beat until combined.

2   Using a metal spoon, add the flour, bicarbonate of soda and cocoa powder and mix to a soft dough. Roll level tablespoons of the mixture into balls. Place the dough balls on the prepared trays and flatten with a fork in a crisscross pattern. Bake for 15–20 minutes. Leave the biscuits to cool for 5 minutes before transferring to wire racks. Allow the biscuits to cool completely before decorating.

3   Place the white chocolate melts in a small heatproof bowl. Stand over a saucepan of simmering water, making sure the bottom of the bowl does not touch the water, and stir until the chocolate is melted and smooth. Dip one-third of each cookie in the white chocolate. Place on a wire rack to set. Melt the dark chocolate melts in the same way, and dip the opposite one-third of each cookie in the melted chocolate, leaving a plain band in the centre.

STORAGE: *These cookies may be stored for up to 3 days in an airtight container.*

HINTS: *Before the chocolate sets, sprinkle the cookies with crushed nuts, if desired. Crunchy or smooth peanut butter may be used, as preferred.*

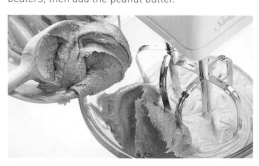
Beat the butter, sugar and egg together with electric beaters, then add the peanut butter.

Place the dough balls on the tray. Press each one with a fork, leaving a crisscross pattern.

After the white chocolate has set, dip the cookies into the melted dark chocolate.

Afghans

PREPARATION TIME: 20 MINUTES | TOTAL COOKING TIME: 20 MINUTES | MAKES 25

150 g (5½ oz) unsalted butter, softened
60 g (2¼ oz/⅓ cup) lightly packed soft brown sugar
1 egg, lightly beaten
1 teaspoon vanilla essence
125 g (4½ oz/1 cup) plain (all-purpose) flour
2 tablespoons unsweetened cocoa powder
30 g (1 oz/⅓ cup) desiccated coconut
45 g (1½ oz/1½ cups) cornflakes, lightly crushed
90 g (3¼ oz/½ cup) dark chocolate chips

1   Preheat the oven to 180°C (350°F/Gas 4). Line two baking trays with baking paper.

2   Using electric beaters, cream the butter and sugar in a large mixing bowl until light and fluffy. Add the egg and vanilla and beat well.

3   Add the sifted flour and cocoa powder to the bowl with the coconut and cornflakes. Stir with a metal spoon until the ingredients are just combined. Put level tablespoons of mixture on the prepared trays, allowing room for spreading. Bake for 20 minutes, or until lightly browned, then leave on the tray to cool completely.

4   Place the chocolate chips in a small heatproof bowl. Bring a saucepan of water to the boil, then remove the pan from the heat. Sit the bowl over the pan, making sure the base of the bowl does not sit in the water. Stir until the chocolate has melted and the mixture is smooth. Spread the top of each biscuit thickly with the melted chocolate and allow to set.

Add the dry ingredients to the mixture and gently stir together with a metal spoon.

Drop level tablespoons of the mixture onto the prepared baking trays.

Spread the melted chocolate thickly across the top of each biscuit.

Choc-vanilla creams

PREPARATION TIME: 45 MINUTES | TOTAL COOKING TIME: 10 MINUTES | MAKES 10

125 g (4½ oz) unsalted butter
40 g (1½ oz/⅓ cup) icing (confectioners') sugar
175 g (6 oz/1½ cups) plain (all-purpose) flour
2 tablespoons unsweetened cocoa powder
120 g (4¼ oz/⅔ cup) chocolate sprinkles
2 teaspoons icing (confectioners') sugar, to dust

VANILLA CREAM
75 g (2½ oz) unsalted butter
85 g (3 oz/⅔ cup) icing (confectioners') sugar
1 teaspoon vanilla essence

1   Preheat the oven to 180°C (350°F/Gas 4). Line a baking tray with baking paper. Using electric beaters, beat the butter and sugar in a small mixing bowl until light and creamy. Using a metal spoon, fold in the sifted flour and cocoa and mix to a soft dough. Roll mixture into balls using 2 teaspoons at a time. Using the base of a glass, press into 4 cm (1½ inch) rounds. Place on the prepared tray. Bake for 10 minutes. Transfer to a wire rack to cool before decorating.

2   To make the vanilla cream, beat the butter and sugar until light and creamy. Add the vanilla and beat until well combined.

3   To assemble the biscuits, spread one biscuit with the vanilla cream and place another on top. Spread vanilla cream around the join.

4   Place the chocolate sprinkles on a plate and roll each biscuit on the side to coat the join. Dust with the icing sugar.

STORAGE: *Store for 2 days in an airtight container.*

Roll the dough into balls and place at well-spaced intervals on the prepared baking tray.

Spread the bottom of one biscuit with the vanilla cream and place another on top.

Roll the assembled biscuit in chocolate sprinkles, making sure the join is well covered.

Almond cinnamon biscuits

PREPARATION TIME: 30 MINUTES | TOTAL COOKING TIME: 12 MINUTES | MAKES 60

200 g (7 oz) blanched almonds
90 g (3¼ oz/⅓ cup) caster (superfine) sugar
40 g (1½ oz/⅓ cup) icing (confectioners')
    sugar
3 teaspoons ground cinnamon
    (see VARIATIONS)
100 g (3½ oz/¾ cup) plain (all-purpose) flour
30 g (1 oz/¼ cup) self-raising flour
2 egg whites

VANILLA ICING (see VARIATIONS)
210 g (7½ oz/1⅔ cups) icing (confectioners')
    sugar
1 egg white, lightly beaten
½ teaspoon vanilla essence

1   Preheat the oven to 150°C (300°F/Gas 2). Line two baking trays with baking paper. Place the almonds, sugars, cinnamon and flours in a food processor. Process for 30 seconds, or until the mixture resembles fine breadcrumbs. Add the egg whites and process for 30 seconds, or until a soft dough forms.

2   Turn the dough onto a lightly floured surface. Knead for 1 minute and shape the dough into a ball. Roll the dough between two sheets of plastic wrap to 5 mm (¼ inch) thickness. Cut into shapes, using a 4 cm (1½ inch) plain or star cookie cutter and place on the prepared trays. Bake for 12 minutes, or until the biscuits are lightly browned. Transfer the biscuits to a wire rack to cool completely.

3   To make the vanilla icing (frosting), sift the icing sugar into a small bowl. Make a well in the centre and add the combined egg white and vanilla essence. Beat the mixture constantly with a wooden spoon until all the icing sugar is incorporated and a firm paste is formed. Using a flat-bladed knife, spread the biscuits with icing. Leave to set.

STORAGE: *These biscuits may be stored in an airtight container for up to 2 days.*

VARIATIONS: *Use 1 teaspoon ground nutmeg instead of cinnamon in the biscuits. Spread the biscuits with lemon icing instead of vanilla, if preferred. Simply add 2 teaspoons of finely grated lemon zest in place of the vanilla essence.*

Place the dry ingredients in a food processor and process for 30 seconds before adding the egg whites.

Using a fluted cookie cutter, cut out shapes and place on the prepared baking trays.

After the biscuits have cooled on a wire rack, spread with the vanilla icing.

Lemon and lime biscuits

PREPARATION TIME: 30 MINUTES + 1 HOUR REFRIGERATION I TOTAL COOKING TIME: 10–15 MINUTES I MAKES 30

150 g (5½ oz) unsalted butter, softened
190 g (6¾ oz/¾ cup) caster (superfine) sugar
1 egg, lightly beaten
1 tablespoon lime juice
2 teaspoons grated lime zest
2 teaspoons grated lemon zest
200 g (7 oz/1⅔ cups) plain (all-purpose) flour
60 g (2¼ oz) marzipan, grated
silver cachous, to decorate

LIME ICING
125 g (4½ oz/1 cup) icing (confectioners')
    sugar, sifted
1 teaspoon finely grated lime zest
1 tablespoon lime juice

1   Line two baking trays with baking paper.
Using electric beaters, beat the butter and sugar
in a large mixing bowl until light and creamy.
Add the egg, lime juice and lime and lemon zest.
Beat until the mixture is well combined.

2   Add the flour and marzipan and, using a
flat-bladed knife, mix until a soft dough forms.
Divide the mixture in two, then turn one portion
out onto a lightly floured surface and press
together until smooth.

3   Roll the biscuit dough into a log shape about
4 cm (1½ inch) in diameter. Cover with plastic
wrap and refrigerate for 1 hour. Repeat with the
remaining dough. Preheat the oven to 180°C
(350°F/Gas 4). Cut the dough roll into 1 cm
(½ inch) slices. Place on the prepared baking
trays and bake for 10–15 minutes, or until lightly
golden. Cool on the trays.

4   To make the lime icing (frosting),
combine the icing sugar, lime zest and juice
and 2 teaspoons water in a small bowl. Beat
the mixture until smooth then either dip the
biscuits in the icing or pipe it on with a piping
(icing) bag. Decorate with silver cachous.

STORAGE: *Store the biscuits in an airtight
container for up to 4 days.*

Turn the dough out onto a lightly floured surface
and press together until smooth.

Using a sharp knife, carefully cut each chilled
dough log into slices.

Orange poppy seed cookies

PREPARATION TIME: 30 MINUTES | TOTAL COOKING TIME: 10 MINUTES | MAKES 30

75 g (2½ oz) unsalted butter
185 g (6½ oz/¾ cup) caster (superfine) sugar
1 egg
1½ teaspoons finely grated orange zest
2 teaspoons orange juice
200 g (7 oz/1⅔ cups) plain (all-purpose) flour
35 g (1¼ oz/¼ cup) cornflour (cornstarch)
¼ teaspoon bicarbonate of soda (baking soda)
1 tablespoon buttermilk
2 tablespoons poppy seeds
185 g (6½ oz/1¼ cups) white chocolate melts
    (buttons)

1   Preheat the oven to 180°C (350°F/Gas 4).
Line two baking trays with baking paper. Using
electric beaters, beat the butter, sugar and egg in a
small mixing bowl until light and creamy. Add the
orange zest and juice and beat until combined.
Transfer the mixture to a medium bowl.

2   Add the sifted flour, cornflour, bicarbonate of
soda, buttermilk and poppy seeds. Using a metal
spoon, mix to a soft dough.

3   Drop mixture, 2 teaspoons at a time, onto the
prepared trays. Press a white chocolate melt into
the centre of each cookie. Bake for 10 minutes,
or until just golden. Cool the cookies on trays
for 5 minutes before transferring to a wire rack
to cool completely.

STORAGE: *Cookies may be stored for up to
3 days in an airtight container.*

HINT: *These cookies are also delicious if topped
with an orange glaze icing, if desired.*

Beat the butter, sugar and egg until light and
creamy then add the orange zest and juice.

Using a metal spoon, fold in the flours, soda,
buttermilk and poppy seeds until well combined.

Firmly press a white chocolate melt into the centre
of each cookie before baking.

Passionfruit melting moments

PREPARATION TIME: 40 MINUTES | TOTAL COOKING TIME: 20 MINUTES | MAKES 14

250 g (9 oz) unsalted butter
40 g (1½ oz/⅓ cup) icing (confectioners')
    sugar
1 teaspoon vanilla essence
185 g (6½ oz/1½ cups) self-raising flour
60 g (2¼ oz/½ cup) custard powder

PASSIONFRUIT FILLING
60 g (2¼ oz) unsalted butter
60 g (2¼ oz/½ cup) icing (confectioners')
    sugar
1½ tablespoons passionfruit pulp

1   Preheat the oven to 180°C (350°F/
Gas 4). Line two baking trays with baking
paper. Place the butter and icing sugar in
a large mixing bowl and beat until light
and creamy. Add the vanilla and beat until
combined. Sift in the flour and custard powder
and mix to a soft dough. Roll level tablespoons
of mixture into 28 balls and place on the
prepared trays. Flatten slightly with a fork.

2   Bake for 20 minutes, or until lightly golden.
Cool on a wire rack.

3   To make the filling, beat the butter and
icing sugar until light and creamy. Fold in the
passionfruit pulp until well combined. Use
the filling to sandwich the biscuits together
and leave to firm before serving.

STORAGE: *The biscuits will keep for up to
4 days in an airtight container.*

VARIATION: *You can vary the flavour of the
filling. For example, to make a coffee filling
dissolve 2 teaspoons instant coffee in 2 teaspoons
water and add to the butter and sugar mixture.
Beat until well combined.*

Beat the butter and sugar together until creamy, then add the vanilla.

Roll the mixture into balls, place on the prepared baking trays and flatten with a fork.

Beat together the butter and icing sugar, then add the passionfruit pulp.

Citrus cookies

PREPARATION TIME: 20 MINUTES I TOTAL COOKING TIME: 15 MINUTES I MAKES ABOUT 30

125 g (4½ oz) unsalted butter
90 g (3¼ oz/¾ cup) icing (confectioners')
    sugar, sifted
185 g (6½ oz/1½ cups) plain (all-purpose) flour
2 teaspoons finely grated lime zest
2 teaspoons finely grated lemon zest
80 g (2¾ oz/⅓ cup) sour cream
1 tablespoon lemon juice

ORANGE ICING
150 g (5½ oz/1¼ cups) icing (confectioners')
    sugar
2 teaspoons finely grated orange zest
2 tablespoons orange juice

1   Preheat the oven to 180°C (350°F/Gas 4).
Lightly grease two baking trays. Place the butter,
icing sugar, flour and lime and lemon zest in a
food processor. Process for 10 seconds or until
the mixture resembles fine breadcrumbs. Add
the sour cream and lemon juice and process for
10 seconds or until the mixture is well combined.

2   Drop level tablespoons of mixture onto the
prepared trays, allowing room for spreading.
Bake for 15 minutes, or until lightly golden. Cool
completely on a wire rack.

3   To make the orange icing (frosting), combine
the icing sugar, zest and juice in a bowl. Stand
the bowl over a pan of simmering water, stirring
until the icing is smooth and glossy. Spread the
icing over the cookies with a flat-bladed knife.

STORAGE: *Store for 3 days in an airtight container
or up to 2 months in the freezer, without icing.*

Process the butter and dry ingredients first, then
add the sour cream and lemon juice.

Remove the cookies from the oven and set aside on
a wire rack to cool.

Work quickly with the icing as overbeating will make
it dull, flat and grainy.

Apple and cinnamon oatcakes

PREPARATION TIME: 20 MINUTES I TOTAL COOKING TIME: 15–20 MINUTES I MAKES ABOUT 20

90 g (3¼ oz/1 cup) chopped dried apple
(see VARIATION)
125 ml (4 fl oz/½ cup) boiling water
125 g (4½ oz) unsalted butter
95 g (3¼ oz/½ cup) lightly packed soft brown
sugar
1 egg, lightly beaten
75 g (2½ oz/¾ cup) rolled (porridge) oats
25 g (1 oz/¼ cup) desiccated coconut
125 g (4½ oz/1 cup) plain (all-purpose) flour,
sifted
1 tablespoon cinnamon sugar (see HINT)

1   Preheat the oven to 180°C (350°F/Gas 4).
Lightly grease two baking trays. Combine the
apple and water in a small bowl and stand for
5 minutes, or until all the water is absorbed.
Using electric beaters, beat the butter and sugar
in a small mixing bowl until light and creamy.
Add the egg and beat well.

2   Transfer the mixture to a large mixing bowl
and add the oats, coconut, apple and flour. Using
a metal spoon, stir until just combined.

3   Drop heaped tablespoons of the mixture
onto the prepared trays, making sure to allow
room for spreading during baking. Sprinkle with
the cinnamon sugar. Bake for 15–20 minutes, or
until the biscuits are lightly golden. Transfer to
wire racks to cool.

STORAGE: *Store for up to 2 days in an airtight
container or freeze for 2 months.*

VARIATION: *Use chopped dried apricots instead
of dried apples.*

HINT: *You can buy cinnamon sugar in the
supermarket, or simply make your own by
combining equal quantities of caster sugar and
ground cinnamon.*

Fold the oats, coconut, apple and flour into the
mixture using a metal spoon.

Make sure the balls of mixture are well spaced as
they will spread during baking.

Raspberry coconut biscuits

PREPARATION TIME: 40 MINUTES | TOTAL COOKING TIME: 10 MINUTES | MAKES 24

BISCUIT PASTRY

60 g (2¼ oz) unsalted butter

125 g (4½ oz/½ cup) caster (superfine) sugar

1 egg

220 g (7¾ oz/1¾ cups) plain (all-purpose)
flour, sifted

ICING

100 g (3½ oz) packet pink marshmallows
(see VARIATION)

40 g (1½ oz) unsalted butter

40 g (1½ oz/¼ cup) icing (confectioners')
sugar, sifted

45 g (1½ oz/½ cup) desiccated coconut

100 g (3½ oz/⅓ cup) raspberry jam
(see VARIATION)

1 Preheat the oven to 180°C (350°F/Gas 4). Line two baking trays with baking paper. To make the pastry, beat the butter and sugar with electric beaters in a small mixing bowl until light and creamy. Transfer to a large mixing bowl. Add the egg and beat until combined. Using a metal spoon, fold in the flour. Turn the dough onto a lightly floured surface. Knead gently for 1 minute or until smooth. Roll out the dough between sheets of baking paper until 5 mm (¼ inch) thick. Using a cutting wheel, cut the dough into 6 x 4.5 cm (2½ x 1¾ inch) rectangles, and place on the prepared trays, allowing room for spreading. Re-roll remaining pastry and repeat cutting. Bake for 10 minutes, or until lightly golden. Transfer to a wire rack when cool.

2 To make the icing (frosting), place the marshmallows and butter in a small saucepan, and stir over low heat until smooth. Stir in the icing sugar and mix until smooth. Place the coconut on a sheet of baking paper. Working very quickly, spread about 1 teaspoon of icing along each side of the biscuit, leaving a strip for the jam in the centre. Dip the iced biscuit into the desiccated coconut and shake off any excess.

3 Place jam in small pan and heat gently until thinned and warm. Using a teaspoon, spread a little jam down the centre of each biscuit.

STORAGE: *Biscuits can be stored for 3 days in a single layer in an airtight container.*

VARIATION: *For a totally different look, use white marshmallows and apricot jam.*

Spread the icing down the sides of the biscuits, then quickly coat with coconut.

Using a teaspoon, fill the centre strip of the biscuits with warmed raspberry jam. Leave to set.

Mocha hazelnut crescents

PREPARATION TIME: 40 MINUTES | TOTAL COOKING TIME: 10 MINUTES | MAKES 24

150 g (5½ oz) unsalted butter
60 g (2¼ oz/¼ cup) caster (superfine) sugar
200 g (7 oz/1⅔ cups) plain (all purpose) flour
2 teaspoons instant coffee
250 g (9 oz) dark chocolate, chopped
    (see HINT)
25 g (1 oz/¼ cup) ground hazelnuts
    (see VARIATION)

1   Preheat the oven to 180°C (350°F/Gas 4). Line two baking trays with baking paper. Using electric beaters, beat the butter and sugar in a large mixing bowl until light and creamy. Sift the flour over the mixing bowl, and using a metal spoon, fold in with the coffee. Mix until a soft dough forms.

2   Shape the mixture into crescents using 1 tablespoon at a time. Place on the prepared trays, and bake for 10 minutes or until golden. Transfer to a wire rack and allow to cool completely before decorating.

3   Place the chocolate in a small heatproof bowl. Stand over a pan of simmering water and stir until the chocolate is melted and the mixture is smooth. Cool slightly.

4   Working with one at a time, place a crescent into the melted chocolate. Using a spoon, carefully coat the whole crescent in chocolate and lift out on a fork, allowing any excess chocolate to drain away. Place on a wire rack, and sprinkle half the top of the crescent with hazelnuts before the chocolate sets. Repeat with the remaining crescents.

STORAGE: *Store biscuits in an airtight container for up to 3 days.*

VARIATION: *Use ground almonds, walnuts or other ground nuts of your choice in place of the hazelnuts, if preferred.*

HINT: *If the weather is warm, use 250 g (9 oz) dark cooking chocolate or dark chocolate melts (buttons) in place of the dark chocolate. Cooking chocolate will set at room temperature.*

Shape the mixture into crescent-shaped biscuits and place on the prepared baking trays.

Melt the chocolate by putting it in a heatproof bowl over a saucepan of simmering water.

Choc-chestnut creams

PREPARATION TIME: 30 MINUTES I TOTAL COOKING TIME: 12 MINUTES I MAKES 30

125 g (4½ oz/1 cup) plain (all-purpose) flour
1 teaspoon unsweetened cocoa powder
¼ teaspoon ground cinnamon
50 g (1¾ oz) unsalted butter
90 g (3¼ oz/⅓ cup) caster (superfine) sugar
1 egg
200 g (7 oz) chocolate chips
1 tablespoon vegetable oil

CHESTNUT CREAM FILLING
125 g (4½ oz) cream cheese
80 g (2¾ oz/¼ cup) sweetened chestnut spread

1 Preheat the oven to 180°C (350°F/Gas 4). Line two baking trays with baking paper. Place the flour, cocoa powder and cinnamon in a food processor. Add the butter and sugar and process until the mixture resembles fine breadcrumbs. Add the egg and process for a further 15 seconds or until a soft dough forms.

2 Turn the dough onto a lightly floured surface and knead for 1 minute until smooth. Roll out to 5 mm (¼ inch) thickness. Cut into 4 cm (1½ inch) rounds, using a fluted cookie cutter. Place on prepared trays. Bake for 12 minutes, or until lightly golden. Cool on trays.

3 Place chocolate chips into a small heatproof bowl. Stand over a saucepan of simmering water, making sure the base does not touch the water, and stir until the chocolate is melted. Remove from the heat. Add the oil and beat until the mixture is smooth. Cool slightly.

4 To make the chestnut cream filling, beat the cream cheese until light and creamy. Add the chestnut spread and beat for 1 minute or until well combined. Spoon the filling into a piping (icing) bag fitted with a fluted piping nozzle and pipe a rosette onto each biscuit. Dip each biscuit into the melted chocolate, coating the filling and top only. Place on a wire rack to set.

STORAGE: *Store biscuits in an airtight container for up to 2 days.*

Using a fluted cookie cutter, cut the dough into round shapes and place on the prepared trays.

Pipe a rosette of chestnut cream filling onto each biscuit, then dip in the melted chocolate.

Coffee kisses

PREPARATION TIME: 30 MINUTES | TOTAL COOKING TIME: 10 MINUTES | MAKES ABOUT 40

375 g (13 oz/3 cups) self-raising flour
160 g (5½ oz) unsalted butter, chopped
125 g (4½ oz/½ cup) caster (superfine) sugar
1 egg, lightly beaten
1 tablespoon instant coffee
1–2 tablespoons iced water
100 g (3½ oz) white chocolate, melted

COFFEE BUTTERCREAM
80 g (2¾ oz) unsalted butter
125 g (4½ oz/1 cup) icing (confectioners')
 sugar, sifted
2 teaspoons water
2 teaspoons instant coffee

1 Preheat the oven to 180°C (350°F/Gas 4). Grease two baking trays and line with baking paper. Sift the flour into a large bowl. Add the butter and rub into the flour, using your fingertips, until it resembles fine breadcrumbs. Add combined sugar, egg and coffee, dissolved in the water, all at once. Mix with a flat-bladed knife until ingredients come together to form a soft dough. Lightly knead until smooth.

2 Roll out the dough between two sheets of baking paper to 5 mm (¼ inch) thickness. Cut into 5 cm (2 inch) rounds, using a fluted cookie cutter. Place on the prepared trays and bake for 10 minutes, or until lightly golden. Transfer the biscuits to a wire rack to cool.

3 To make the coffee buttercream, using electric beaters, beat the butter and icing sugar until light and creamy. Add the combined water and coffee and beat until combined. Place the mixture in a piping (icing) bag fitted with a fluted nozzle and pipe buttercream onto half of the biscuits. Top with another biscuit and sandwich together. Drizzle or pipe with white melted chocolate.

Remove the cooked biscuits from the oven and transfer to a wire rack to completely cool.

Using a piping (icing) bag with a fluted nozzle, pipe the coffee buttercream onto the biscuits.

Cornflake cookies

PREPARATION TIME: 15 MINUTES | TOTAL COOKING TIME: 20 MINUTES | MAKES 36

125 g (4½ oz) unsalted butter, softened
185 g (6½ oz/¾ cup) sugar
2 eggs, lightly beaten
1 teaspoon vanilla essence
2 tablespoons currants
135 g (4¾ oz/1½ cups) desiccated coconut
½ teaspoon bicarbonate of soda (baking soda)
½ teaspoon baking powder
250 g (9 oz/2 cups) plain (all-purpose) flour
90 g (3¼ oz/3 cups) cornflakes, lightly crushed
  (see NOTE)

1 Preheat the oven to 180°C (350°F/Gas 4). Line two baking trays with baking paper.

2 Cream the butter and sugar in a small bowl with electric beaters until light and fluffy. Add the eggs a little at a time, beating thoroughly after each addition. Add the vanilla and beat until well combined.

3 Transfer the mixture to a large bowl and stir in the currants and coconut. Fold in the sifted bicarbonate of soda, baking powder and flour with a metal spoon and stir until the mixture is almost smooth. Put the cornflakes in a shallow dish, drop level tablespoons of mixture onto the cornflakes and roll into balls. Arrange on the trays, allowing room for spreading.

4 Bake for 15–20 minutes, or until crisp and golden. Cool slightly on the tray, then transfer to a wire rack to cool. When completely cold, store in an airtight container.

NOTE: *A mess-free method for crushing cornflakes is to put them in a plastic bag and lightly crush with your hands or a rolling pin.*

Add the beaten eggs gradually to the mixture, making sure they are well combined.

Roll balls of the mixture in the crushed cornflakes on a piece of baking paper.

Pecan maple shortbreads

PREPARATION TIME: 30 MINUTES | TOTAL COOKING TIME: 20 MINUTES | MAKES ABOUT 20

125 g (4½ oz/1 cup) plain (all-purpose) flour
60 g (2¼ oz/½ cup) ground pecans
2 tablespoons icing (confectioners') sugar
90 g (3¼ oz) unsalted butter, chopped
2 tablespoons maple syrup
50 g (1¾ oz/⅓ cup) white chocolate melts
   (buttons), melted

1   Preheat the oven to 180°C (350°F/Gas 4).
Line a baking tray with baking paper. Place the
flour, pecans, icing sugar and butter in a food
processor and process for 1 minute or until the
mixture comes together.

2   Turn onto a lightly floured surface, and press
together to form a smooth dough. Roll out on
a sheet of baking paper to a thickness of 5 mm
(¼ inch). Using a 4 cm (1½ inch) heart-shaped
cutter, cut out shapes.

3   Transfer to the prepared tray, bake for
10 minutes and remove from the oven. Brush
each shortbread generously with the maple syrup
and bake for another 8–10 minutes. Transfer to
a wire rack to cool completely. Spoon the white
chocolate into a small piping (icing) bag and pipe
around the edge of the biscuits.

STORAGE: *Store for up to 4 days in an airtight*
container in cool, dark place.

Place the flour, pecans, icing sugar and butter into a food processor.

Roll the dough out on a lightly floured surface and cut out shapes.

Place the shortbreads on the prepared baking tray and brush with maple syrup.

Passionfruit shortbread

PREPARATION TIME: 45 MINUTES I TOTAL COOKING TIME: 20 MINUTES I MAKES ABOUT 40

250 g (9 oz) unsalted butter
90 g (3¼ oz/⅓ cup) caster (superfine) sugar
280 g (10 oz/2¼ cups) plain (all-purpose) flour
45 g (1½ oz/¼ cup) rice flour

PASSIONFRUIT ICING
310 g (11 oz/2½ cups) icing (confectioners') sugar, sifted
4 tablespoons fresh or tinned passionfruit pulp
40 g (1½ oz) unsalted butter, softened

1 Preheat the oven to 160°C (315°F/Gas 2–3). Line two baking trays with baking paper. Using electric beaters, beat the butter and sugar in a small mixing bowl until light and creamy. Fold in the sifted flours and mix until a soft dough forms. Turn out onto a lightly floured surface. Knead gently for 1 minute or until smooth.

2 Roll out the dough between two sheets of baking paper to 5 mm (¼ inch) thickness. Cut into 4 x 4 cm (1½ x 1½ inch) diamonds. Place on prepared trays, allowing room for spreading. Re-roll the remaining dough and cut out diamonds until all the dough is used. Bake for 15 minutes, or until lightly brown. Stand for 5 minutes, then cool on a wire rack.

3 To make the passionfruit icing, combine the icing sugar, passionfruit pulp, butter and 2 tablespoons water in a bowl to form a smooth paste. Stand the bowl in a saucepan of simmering water, stirring until the icing is smooth and glossy.

4 Remove the pan from the heat but leave the bowl of icing to stand in the warm water while icing the biscuits. Spread each diamond with ½ teaspoon of icing.

STORAGE: *These biscuits can be stored in an airtight container for up to 2 days.*

NOTE: *Overheating the icing will make it dull and grainy. Try to work as quickly as possible and dip the knife into hot water occasionally to give the icing a smooth finish.*

Use a ruler or other straight edge as a cutting guide to keep your lines straight.

After the biscuits have cooled, use a flat-bladed knife to spread the icing.

Ginger pecan biscotti

PREPARATION TIME: 30 MINUTES + 30 MINUTES COOLING | TOTAL COOKING TIME: 1 HOUR | MAKES ABOUT 20

100 g (3½ oz/1 cup) pecans
2 eggs
155 g (5½ oz/⅔ cup) firmly packed soft brown
  sugar
50 g (1¾ oz/½ cup) self-raising flour
175 g (6 oz/1½ cups) plain (all-purpose) flour
100 g (3½ oz) glacé (candied) ginger, finely
  chopped

1 Preheat the oven to 160°C (315°F/Gas 2–3).
Spread the pecans onto a baking tray and bake
for 10–12 minutes, or until toasted. Tip the
pecans onto a board to cool, then roughly chop.
Line the baking tray with baking paper.

2 Using electric beaters, beat the eggs and sugar
in a large mixing bowl until pale and creamy.
Sift the flours into the bowl, add the pecans and
glacé ginger. Mix to a soft dough, then place onto
a prepared tray and shape into a 23 x 9 cm (9 x
3½ inch) loaf.

3 Bake for 35–40 minutes, or until lightly
golden. Cool on a wire rack for 15 minutes each
side, then cut into 1 cm (½ inch) slices with a
serrated bread knife. The biscotti will be crumbly
on the edges so work slowly and, if possible, try
to hold the sides as you cut. Arrange slices in a
single layer on baking trays. Bake for 10 minutes
each side. Don't worry if they don't seem fully
dry as they will become crisp on cooling.

STORAGE: *Cool completely before storing in an
airtight container for 2–3 weeks.*

Add the nuts and ginger and mix until the mixture
becomes a soft dough.

Place the dough on the prepared baking tray and
shape into a log.

Using a large serrated bread knife, carefully cut the
log into slices.

Ginger shortbread creams

PREPARATION TIME: 25 MINUTES | TOTAL COOKING TIME: 15 MINUTES | MAKES 12

140 g (5 oz) plain (all-purpose) flour
2 tablespoons cornflour (cornstarch)
100 g (3½ oz) unsalted butter, chopped
2 tablespoons soft brown sugar

FILLING
60 g (2¼ oz) unsalted butter
40 g (1½ oz/⅓ cup) icing (confectioners') sugar
1 tablespoon finely chopped glacé (candied)
    ginger

1   Preheat the oven to 180°C (350°F/Gas 4).
Line two baking trays with baking paper. Place
the flours, butter and sugar in a food processor.
Process until the mixture forms a dough. Turn
out onto a lightly floured surface and knead for
20 seconds or until smooth.

2   Roll level teaspoons of the mixture into balls.
Place on the prepared trays and press with a fork
in a crisscross pattern. Bake for 12–15 minutes,
until just golden. Transfer the biscuits to a wire
rack to cool completely before filling.

3   To make the filling, beat the butter and icing
sugar until light and fluffy. Add the ginger and
beat until combined. Spread half the biscuits
with the filling and sandwich with the plain ones.

STORAGE: *This shortbread can be stored for up
to 3 days in an airtight container.*

VARIATION: *Add 1 teaspoon of ground ginger to
the biscuit mixture.*

Process the flours, butter and sugar for 30 seconds
or until a dough forms.

Roll the dough into balls and place on the prepared
baking trays, allowing room for spreading.

After the biscuits have cooled, sandwich them
together with the ginger filling.

Choc-mint swirls

PREPARATION TIME: 30 MINUTES | TOTAL COOKING TIME: 15 MINUTES | MAKES 30

65 g (2¼ oz) unsalted butter
60 g (2¼ oz/¼ cup) caster (superfine) sugar
140 g (5 oz) plain (all-purpose) flour
2 tablespoons unsweetened cocoa powder
1–2 tablespoons milk
30 chocolate chips

TOPPING
100 g (3½ oz) unsalted butter, extra
165 g (5¾ oz/1⅓ cups) icing (confectioners')
    sugar
few drops peppermint essence

1   Preheat the oven to 180°C (350°F/Gas 4).
Line two baking trays with baking paper. Using
electric beaters, beat the butter and sugar in a
small mixing bowl until light and creamy. Add
the sifted flour and cocoa and the milk. Stir
with a flat-bladed knife until the mixture forms
a soft dough. Turn out onto a piece of baking
paper and knead for 1 minute or until smooth.

2   Roll the dough out to a 5 mm (¼ inch)
thickness. Cut the dough into rounds, using a
4 cm (1½ inch) plain cookie cutter. Place on
the prepared trays and bake for 15 minutes.
Transfer to a wire rack to cool completely
before decorating.

3   To make the topping, beat the butter with
electric beaters until soft. Add the icing sugar
and beat until smooth, creamy and light. Add
the peppermint essence to taste and beat until
combined. Using a piping (icing) bag fitted with
a large fluted nozzle, carefully pipe a rosette of
peppermint cream onto each biscuit. Place a
chocolate chip in the centre of each rosette.

STORAGE: *Store for up to 2 days in an airtight
container in a cool, dark place.*

VARIATION: *Dust the choc-mint swirls with
1 teaspoon each of icing sugar and cocoa powder,
sifted together.*

Sift the flour and cocoa powder into the mixture, add
the milk and combine with a flat-bladed knife.

Place the rounds at well-spaced intervals on the
baking trays to allow for spreading during baking.

Pipe the peppermint cream onto each biscuit and
top with a chocolate chip.

Cats' tongues

PREPARATION TIME: 20 MINUTES | TOTAL COOKING TIME: 8 MINUTES | MAKES 40

80 g (2¾ oz) unsalted butter, chopped
80 g (2¾ oz/⅔ cup) icing (confectioners')
    sugar, plus extra, to dust
2 egg whites
2 tablespoons caster (superfine) sugar
90 g (3¼ oz/¾ cup) plain (all-purpose) flour

1   Preheat the oven to 180°C (350°F/Gas 4).
Lightly grease a baking tray and line the base
with baking paper. Grease the baking paper.
Using electric beaters, beat the butter and sifted
icing sugar in a small bowl until light and fluffy.
Transfer the mixture to a large bowl.

2   In a separate bowl, using electric beaters, beat
the egg whites until firm peaks form. Add the
sugar gradually, beating until the mixture is thick
and glossy and all the sugar is dissolved. Using a
metal spoon, fold the egg mixture into the butter
mixture. Add the sifted flour and fold in quickly
and lightly, making sure not to overmix.

3   Spoon the mixture into a piping (icing) bag
fitted with a 1 cm (½ inch) piping nozzle. Pipe
the mixture into 8 cm (3¼ inch) lengths onto the
prepared tray, allowing room for spreading.

4   Bake for 8 minutes, or until lightly golden.
Leave the biscuits to stand on the tray for
1 minute, then cool completely on a wire rack.
Dust with icing sugar.

STORAGE: *Store biscuits in an airtight container
for up to 2 days.*

VARIATION: *Add ½ teaspoon finely grated
orange or lemon zest to the mixture, if desired.*

Fold the beaten egg whites into the butter mixture
with a metal spoon.

Draw guide lines on the baking paper, then turn the
paper over before piping the mixture onto the tray.

Remove the biscuits from the tray with a flat-bladed
knife and leave to cool on a wire rack.

Chocolate cherry oaties

PREPARATION TIME: 12 MINUTES | TOTAL COOKING TIME: 15–20 MINUTES | MAKES 25

100 g (3½ oz/¾ cup) plain (all-purpose) flour
30 g (1 oz/¼ cup) self-raising flour
150 g (5½ oz/1½ cups) rolled (porridge) oats
125 g (4½ oz/½ cup) caster (superfine) sugar
125 g (4½ oz) glacé (candied) cherries,
    quartered
60 g (2¼ oz/½ cup) chopped pecans
45 g (1½ oz/⅓ cup) chocolate chips
60 g (2¼ oz) chopped white chocolate
125 g (4½ oz) unsalted butter, melted
2 eggs, lightly beaten

1 Preheat the oven to 180°C (350°F/Gas 4). Line two baking trays with baking paper. Sift the flours into a large mixing bowl. Add the oats, sugar, cherries, pecans and solid chocolates and stir. Make a well in the centre of the ingredients, then add the butter and eggs.

2 Using a flat-bladed knife, stir until all the ingredients are well combined.

3 Drop heaped tablespoons of the mixture onto the prepared trays, allowing room for spreading during baking. Bake for 15–20 minutes, or until lightly browned. Transfer to a wire rack to cool.

STORAGE: *Store in an airtight container for up to 2 days in cool, dark place.*

Make a well in the centre of the dry ingredients and pour in the melted butter.

Make sure the mixture is well combined by stirring with a flat-bladed knife.

Spoon the mixture, 1 tablespoon at a time, onto the prepared baking trays.

Fruity shortbread pillows

PREPARATION TIME: 1 HOUR + 15 MINUTES REFRIGERATION | TOTAL COOKING TIME: 15–20 MINUTES | MAKES 18

250 g (9 oz/2 cups) plain (all-purpose) flour
60 g (2¼ oz/½ cup) icing (confectioners')
   sugar
185 g (6½ oz) chilled unsalted butter, chopped
1 egg
45 g (1½ oz) fruit mince (mincemeat)
   (see VARIATION)
1 egg, extra, lightly beaten
icing (confectioners') sugar, to serve

1 Preheat the oven to 180°C (350°F/Gas 4). Line two baking trays with baking paper. Place the flour, sugar and butter in a food processor. Process for 20 seconds or until mixture resembles fine breadcrumbs. Add the egg and process for a further 15 seconds or until the mixture comes together. Turn onto a lightly floured surface and knead for 2–3 minutes, or until the dough is smooth. Leave the dough, covered with plastic wrap, in the refrigerator for 10–15 minutes.

2 Divide the pastry in two. Roll one portion on a sheet of baking paper to a 5 mm (¼ inch) thickness. Lightly mark circles with a 4 cm (1½ inch) cutter. Spoon ½ teaspoon of fruit mince into the centre of each circle. Brush the pastry with egg.

3 On a sheet of baking paper, roll the remaining pastry to 2.5 mm (⅛ inch) thickness. (Pastry should be rolled into a slightly larger circle, approximately 1.5 cm (⅝ inch) extra in diameter.) Lift the pastry, using the rolling pin as a lever, over the top of the first pastry sheet. Press down between the filling to seal the edges. Cut the biscuits, using a floured 4 cm (1½ inch) round cutter. Place on the prepared baking trays. Bake for 15–20 minutes, or until pale golden. Cool biscuits on trays. Dust with icing sugar.

STORAGE: *Store the biscuits for up to 3 days in an airtight container.*

VARIATION: *Use 45 g (1½ oz/¼ cup) finely chopped mixed dried fruit, with 2–3 teaspoons of rum, brandy or fruit juice. Mix well and leave to stand until the fruit has absorbed the liquid.*

Mark the pastry with a cookie cutter, then place the fruit mince in the centre of the circles.

Once you have sealed the edges, cut out the biscuits with a round cutter.

Chocolate Jamaican rounds

PREPARATION TIME: 25 MINUTES | TOTAL COOKING TIME: 25 MINUTES | MAKES 30

100 g (3½ oz) unsalted butter
90 g (3¼ oz/⅓ cup) caster (superfine) sugar
1 teaspoon coconut essence
2 tablespoons coconut cream
60 g (2¼ oz) milk chocolate, melted
2 teaspoons grated lime zest
45 g (1½ oz/½ cup) desiccated coconut, plus
    2 tablespoons extra
220 g (7¾ oz/1¾ cups) plain (all-purpose) flour

ICING

30 g (1 oz) unsalted butter
60 g (2¼ oz) dark cooking chocolate, chopped
¼ teaspoon coconut essence
2 teaspoons coconut cream

1   Preheat the oven to 180°C (350°F/Gas 4).
Line two baking trays with baking paper. Using
electric beaters, beat the butter and sugar in a
small mixing bowl until light and creamy. Add
the coconut essence, coconut cream, chocolate
and lime zest and beat until well combined.

2   Add the desiccated coconut and flour and
press together to form a soft dough. Turn onto a
lightly floured surface and knead for 1 minute or
until the dough is smooth.

3   Roll 3 teaspoons of the mixture at a time into
balls. Place on the prepared trays. Flatten the
balls slightly, using the base of a glass. Bake for
20 minutes, or until lightly browned. Leave the
biscuits to cool on the trays.

4   To make the icing (frosting), place the butter
and chocolate in a small heatproof bowl. Stand
over a saucepan of simmering water, making sure
the base does not touch the water, and stir until
the mixture is smooth. Remove from the heat.
Add the coconut essence and coconut cream
and stir to combine. When the biscuits are cool,
dip the tops in the icing. Sprinkle with the extra
coconut and leave to set.

Knead the dough until smooth on a lightly floured
work surface.

Using the base of a glass, slightly flatten the balls
of dough after they are placed on the trays.

Choc-caramel rounds

PREPARATION TIME: 30 MINUTES | TOTAL COOKING TIME: 25 MINUTES | MAKES 30

185 g (6½ oz/1½ cups) plain (all-purpose) flour
1 tablespoon unsweetened cocoa powder
180 g (6 oz) unsalted butter, chopped
95 g (3¼ oz/½ cup) soft brown sugar
1 egg yolk, lightly beaten
2 tablespoons grated milk chocolate
200 g (7 oz/1¼ cups) chocolate chips, plus
    30 chocolate chips, extra

CARAMEL FILLING
200 g (7 oz) jersey caramels, chopped (see
    NOTE)
1 tablespoon unsalted butter
1 tablespoon cream

1   Preheat the oven to 180°C (350°F/Gas 4).
Line two baking trays with baking paper. Sift the
flour and cocoa into a large mixing bowl. Add
the butter and sugar and, using your fingertips,
rub the butter into the flour for 2 minutes, or
until the mixture is fine and crumbly. Add the
egg yolk and grated chocolate and press together
to form a soft dough. Knead on a lightly floured
surface for 1 minute.

2   Roll the pastry to 5 mm (¼ inch) thick.
Using a fluted cookie cutter, cut into 5 cm
(2 inch) rounds and place on the trays. Bake
for 15 minutes or until lightly browned. Put
the biscuits on a wire rack to cool.

3   To make the caramel filling, combine the
caramels, butter and cream in a small saucepan.
Stir over low heat for 3 minutes, or until the
caramels have melted. Remove from the heat
and beat until smooth. Cool.

4   To melt the chocolate chips for the top of the
biscuits, place in a small heatproof bowl. Stand
the bowl over a saucepan of simmering water,
making sure the base does not touch the water,
and stir until the chocolate is melted and smooth.
Spread a little melted chocolate over each biscuit
and place half a teaspoon of filling in the centre.
Push one of the extra chocolate chips on top.

NOTE: Jersey caramels are soft toffee caramels,
available from most supermarkets.

Place the caramel on top of the biscuits after
spreading with melted chocolate.

Push a chocolate chip into the caramel centre until
it is firmly placed.

Sugar and spice palmiers

PREPARATION TIME: 20 MINUTES + 15 MINUTES REFRIGERATION | TOTAL COOKING TIME: 20 MINUTES | MAKES 32

2 tablespoons raw (demerara) sugar
1 teaspoon mixed (pumpkin pie) spice
1 teaspoon ground cinnamon
1 sheet frozen puff pastry, thawed
40 g (1½ oz) unsalted butter, melted

1 Preheat the oven to 210°C (415°F/Gas 6–7). Lightly grease two baking trays and line with baking paper. Combine the sugar and spices in a small mixing bowl. Cut the pastry sheet in half and brush with the melted butter. Sprinkle with the sugar and spice mixture until the pastry sheet is well covered, reserving 2 teaspoons.

2 Fold the long edges of the pastry inwards, then fold again so that the edges almost meet in the centre. Fold once more, place the pastry on a baking tray and refrigerate for 15 minutes. Using a small, sharp knife, cut the pastry pieces into 32 slices.

3 Arrange the palmiers cut side up onto the prepared trays, brush with butter and sprinkle lightly with the reserved sugar and spice mixture. Bake for 20 minutes, or until golden. Transfer to a wire rack to cool completely.

STORAGE: *Store for up to a day in an airtight container. Palmiers may be re-crisped in a 180°C (350°F/Gas 4) oven for 5 minutes before serving.*

Generously sprinkle the sugar and spice mixture over the sheet of puff pastry.

Fold the sides of the pastry inwards and then again so that they almost meet in the centre.

Using a pastry brush, lightly coat the palmiers with melted butter and sprinkle with the sugar mixture.

Choc-hazelnut scrolls

PREPARATION TIME: 25 MINUTES | TOTAL COOKING TIME: 15 MINUTES + 30 MINUTES REFRIGERATION | MAKES 35

250 g (9 oz/2 cups) plain (all-purpose) flour
60 g (2¼ oz/½ cup) ground hazelnuts
100 g (3½ oz) unsalted butter
125 g (4½ oz/½ cup) caster (superfine) sugar
1 egg, lightly beaten
2 tablespoons iced water
80 g (2¾ oz/¼ cup) chocolate hazelnut spread

1 Line two baking trays with baking paper. Place the flour and hazelnuts in a food processor and add the butter and sugar. Process until the mixture resembles fine breadcrumbs. Add the combined egg and water and process until the mixture forms a dough. Turn out onto a lightly floured surface and knead for 30 seconds or until the dough is smooth.

2 Place the dough onto a large sheet of baking paper and roll out into a rectangle of 25 x 35 cm (10 x 14 inch). Trim the edges. Spread the dough evenly with the chocolate hazelnut spread. Using the baking paper to lift the dough, roll up from the long side in Swiss-roll style. Wrap tightly in baking paper and refrigerate for 30 minutes.

3 Preheat the oven to 180°C (350°F/Gas 4). Cut the roll into 1 cm (½ inch) slices, wiping the knife's blade between each cut. Place the slices on the prepared baking trays and bake for 15 minutes or until golden. Transfer to a wire rack to cool.

STORAGE: *Store for up to 3 days in an airtight container in cool, dark place.*

Mix the egg and water in a small bowl and add to the mixture in the food processor.

Spread the dough with chocolate hazelnut spread and then carefully roll up.

Place the dough roll onto a clean work surface and cut into slices.

Scottish shortbread

PREPARATION TIME: 25 MINUTES + 20 MINUTES REFRIGERATION I TOTAL COOKING TIME: 30–35 MINUTES I MAKES TWO 20 CM ROUNDS

275 g (9¾ oz/2¼ cups) plain (all-purpose) flour
125 g (4½ oz/⅔ cup) rice flour
250 g (9 oz) unsalted butter, softened
125 g (4½ oz/½ cup) caster (superfine) sugar
1 teaspoon sugar, to decorate

1 Preheat the oven to 160°C (315°F/Gas 2–3). Line two baking trays with baking paper. Mark a 20 cm (8 inch) circle on the paper on each tray and turn the paper over.

2 Sift the flours into a large mixing bowl and add the butter and sugar. Using your fingertips, rub the butter into the flour mixture until a soft dough forms. Add a pinch of salt and gather together. Divide the dough into two portions, then wrap in plastic wrap and refrigerate for 20 minutes.

3 Place one dough portion on each tray and press into a round, using the drawn circle as a guide. Pinch and flute the edges decoratively and prick the surface with a fork. Use a knife to mark each circle into 12 segments. Sprinkle with the sugar and bake for 30–35 minutes, until firm and pale golden. Leave to cool on the trays then break into scored wedges to serve.

STORAGE: *When completely cold, store the shortbread in an airtight container.*

NOTE: *Usually no liquid is used, but if the dough is very crumbly, add not more than 1 tablespoon of milk or cream.*

Make a circle on the baking paper by tracing around a mixing bowl.

Using your fingertips, rub the butter into the flour mixture until a soft dough forms.

Decorate the edges of the shortbread by pinching the dough.

Coconut macaroons

PREPARATION TIME: 15 MINUTES | TOTAL COOKING TIME: 15–20 MINUTES | MAKES 45

3 egg whites
250 g (9 oz/1 cup) caster (superfine) sugar
½ teaspoon coconut essence
1 teaspoon grated lemon zest
2 tablespoons cornflour (cornstarch), sifted
180 g (6 oz/2 cups) desiccated coconut

1 Preheat the oven to 180°C (350°F/Gas 4). Line two baking trays with baking paper. Place the egg whites in a small dry mixing bowl. Using electric beaters, beat the egg whites until firm peaks form. Add the sugar gradually, beating constantly until the mixture is thick and glossy and all the sugar is dissolved. Add the coconut essence and lemon zest and beat until just combined.

2 Transfer the mixture to a large mixing bowl and add the cornflour and coconut. Using a metal spoon, stir until just combined.

3 Drop 2 level teaspoons of mixture onto the prepared trays about 3 cm (1¼ inch) apart. Bake on the top shelf of the oven for 15–20 minutes, or until golden.

4 Leave the macaroons to cool completely on the trays.

STORAGE: *Store in an airtight container for up to 2 days.*

HINTS: *Sprinkle biscuits with shredded coconut before baking. Drizzle with melted chocolate before serving.*

Fold the cornflour and coconut into the egg white mixture with a metal spoon.

Using a flat-bladed knife and a spoon, shape macaroons out of the mixture.

Jaffa rings

PREPARATION TIME: 30 MINUTES I TOTAL COOKING TIME: 20 MINUTES I MAKES ABOUT 45

180 g (6 oz) unsalted butter
125 g (4½ oz/½ cup) caster (superfine) sugar
1 egg, lightly beaten
1½ teaspoons finely grated orange zest
50 g (1¾ oz) milk chocolate, grated
125 g (4½ oz/1 cup) self-raising flour, sifted
250 g (9 oz/2 cups) plain (all-purpose) flour, sifted
100 g (3½ oz) milk chocolate melts (buttons) (see HINT)

1   Preheat the oven to 180°C (350°F/Gas 4). Line two baking trays with baking paper. Using electric beaters, beat the butter, sugar and egg in a large mixing bowl until light and creamy. Add the orange zest and grated chocolate and beat until well combined.

2   Using a flat-bladed knife, fold in the flours and mix together to form a soft dough. Turn onto a lightly floured surface and knead for 30 seconds or until the dough is smooth.

3   Roll 3 teaspoonfuls of mixture into small oblongs. Continue rolling into lengths of 20 cm (8 inch). Carefully fold in half and twist. Form the twisted rope into a ring. Place on the prepared trays. Bake for 12–15 minutes and transfer to a wire rack to cool.

4   Place the chocolate melts in a small heatproof bowl. Sit over a saucepan of simmering water, making sure the bottom of the bowl does not sit in the water, and stir until the chocolate is melted and smooth. Cool slightly. Dip bases of the biscuits into the melted chocolate. Stand on a wire rack to set.

STORAGE: *Biscuits may be kept for up to 4 days in an airtight container.*

HINT: *To decorate these biscuits quickly, the melted chocolate can be simply drizzled off the end of the prongs of a fork.*

Roll the dough into lengths before folding in half and plaiting together.

Dip the base of the biscuits into the cooled chocolate, then set aside to set.

Chocolate lemon swirls

PREPARATION TIME: 12 MINUTES | TOTAL COOKING TIME: 12–15 MINUTES | MAKES ABOUT 40

125 g (4½ oz) unsalted butter

85 g (3 oz/⅔ cup) icing (confectioners') sugar

1 egg, lightly beaten

2 teaspoons finely grated lemon zest
   (see VARIATION)

155 g (5½ oz/1¼ cups) plain (all-purpose) flour

25 g (1 oz/¼ cup) unsweetened cocoa powder

2 tablespoons mixed peel (mixed candied
   citrus peel)

1 Preheat the oven to 180°C (350°F/Gas 4). Line two baking trays with baking paper. Using electric beaters, beat the butter and icing sugar until light and creamy. Add the egg and lemon zest, and beat until well combined.

2 Add the flour and cocoa. Using a metal spoon, stir until the ingredients are just combined.

3 Spoon the mixture into a piping (icing) bag fitted with a fluted 1 cm (½ inch) piping nozzle and pipe swirls about 3 cm (1¼ inch) in diameter onto the prepared trays. Top each swirl with a few pieces of the mixed peel. Bake for 12–15 minutes. Leave the biscuits to cool on the trays.

STORAGE: *The biscuits may be stored in an airtight container for up to 2 days.*

VARIATION: *Use orange zest in place of the lemon zest, if preferred.*

Add the egg and 2 teaspoons of finely grated lemon zest to the combined butter and sugar.

Sift the flour and cocoa powder into the bowl and stir with a metal spoon.

Pipe swirls of the mixture onto the prepared baking trays and place the mixed peel on top.

Chocolate apricot pretzels

PREPARATION TIME: 25 MINUTES | TOTAL COOKING TIME: 20 MINUTES | MAKES 30

80 g (2¾ oz/½ cup) finely chopped dried
   apricots
80 ml (2½ fl oz/⅓ cup) orange juice
20 g (¾ oz) unsalted butter
120 g (4¼ oz/¾ cup) self-raising flour
75 g (2½ oz/½ cup) plain (all-purpose) flour
60 g (2¼ oz) unsalted butter, chopped
55 g (2 oz/¼ cup) caster (superfine) sugar
2 egg yolks
70 g (2½ oz/½ cup) grated milk chocolate
150 g (5½ oz/1 cup) white chocolate melts
   (buttons)
10 g (¼ oz) white vegetable shortening

1 Preheat the oven to 180°C (350°F/
Gas 4). Line two baking trays with baking
paper. Combine the apricots, juice and butter
in a small saucepan. Stir over low heat for
5 minutes; remove from heat, and cool.

2 Sift the flours into a large mixing bowl.
Add the butter and sugar. Using fingertips,
rub the butter into the flour for 2 minutes, or
until the mixture resembles fine breadcrumbs.
Add the egg yolks, grated chocolate and cooled
apricot mixture. Press the mixture together to
form a soft dough.

3 Turn onto a lightly floured surface and
knead for 2 minutes until smooth. Roll 2 level
teaspoons of mixture at a time into balls. Roll
the dough into 15 cm (6 inch) x 5 mm (¼ inch)
lengths. Shape and loop into pretzels. Bake for
15 minutes, or until lightly browned. Transfer
to a wire rack to cool completely. Combine
the chocolate melts and shortening in a small
saucepan and stir over low heat until melted.
Dip half of each pretzel diagonally into the
melted chocolate mixture.

Combine the apricots, orange juice and butter in a small saucepan and place over a low heat.

Using your fingertips, rub the butter into the flour until the mixture is fine and crumbly.

Shape the rolled lengths of dough into pretzel shapes on a floured work surface.

Orange and almond tuiles

PREPARATION TIME: 30 MINUTES | TOTAL COOKING TIME: 10 MINUTES | MAKES ABOUT 15

90 g (3¼ oz) unsalted butter
90 g (3¼ oz/⅓ cup) caster (superfine) sugar
30 g (1 oz/¼ cup) plain (all-purpose) flour
25 g (1 oz/¼ cup) flaked almonds, crushed
  slightly
1 tablespoon finely chopped mixed peel
  (mixed candied citrus peel)

1 Preheat the oven to 180°C (350°F/Gas 4).
Lightly grease a large baking tray and dust
lightly with flour. Using electric beaters, beat
the butter and sugar in a small mixing bowl
until light and fluffy. Add the flour and stir until
combined. Add the flaked almonds and mixed
peel. Stir until well combined.

2 Cook in batches. Place heaped teaspoonfuls
of the mixture about 10 cm (4 inches) apart on
the prepared tray. Spread each spoonful of the
mixture out into a 5 cm (2 inch) circle. Bake for
10 minutes or until golden.

3 Remove the tray from the oven and stand
for 1 minute. Carefully lift each circle off the tray
with a flat-bladed knife and drape immediately
over a rolling pin to curl. Leave to cool on the
rolling pin. Repeat with the remaining circles.

STORAGE: *Tuiles can be stored in an airtight
container for several days before use.*

HINT: *Cook only about 4–6 tuiles at a time, as
they cool and harden very quickly. Grease and
flour the tray again before baking each batch.*

Beat the butter and sugar with electric beaters until
light and fluffy.

Spread the mixture out into a circle with a flat-bladed
knife and bake for 10 minutes.

Leave the tuiles to cool on the rolling pin and they
will retain their curled shape.

Cocoa sesame biscuits

PREPARATION TIME: 15 MINUTES I TOTAL COOKING TIME: 15 MINUTES I MAKES ABOUT 40

90 g (3¼ oz/¾ cup) plain (all-purpose) flour
25 g (1 oz/¼ cup) unsweetened cocoa powder
75 g (2½ oz/¾ cup) rolled (porridge) oats
150 g (5½ oz/1 cup) sesame seeds
170 g (6 oz/¾ cup) caster (superfine) sugar
100 g (3½ oz) unsalted butter
2 tablespoons golden syrup (if unavailable,
    substitute with half honey and half dark
    corn syrup)
1 tablespoon boiling water
1 teaspoon bicarbonate of soda (baking soda)

1 Preheat the oven to 160°C (315°F/Gas 2–3).
Line two baking trays with baking paper. Sift
the flour and cocoa powder into a large mixing
bowl. Add the rolled oats, sesame seeds and
sugar and combine.

2 Combine the butter and golden syrup in a
saucepan. Stir over a low heat until the butter
is melted and the mixture is smooth. Pour
boiling water into a small mixing bowl, add the
bicarbonate of soda and stir until dissolved.
Add to the golden syrup mixture. Using a metal
spoon, fold the mixture into the dry ingredients
until well combined.

3 Drop 3 level teaspoons of mixture onto the
prepared trays, allowing room for spreading.
Flatten each one slightly with your fingertips.
Bake for 12 minutes, or until lightly golden.
Cool the biscuits on the trays for 5 minutes before
transferring to a wire rack to cool completely.

Combine the flour, cocoa powder, oats, sesame
seeds and sugar in a large mixing bowl.

Fold the golden syrup mixture into the dry
ingredients with a metal spoon.

Make sure the biscuits are well spaced on the
baking trays as they will spread during baking.

Slices

Tipsy currant slice

PREPARATION TIME: 20 MINUTES + 15 MINUTES STANDING | TOTAL COOKING TIME: 25 MINUTES | MAKES 16 PIECES

75 g (2½ oz/½ cup) currants

60 ml (2 fl oz/¼ cup) brandy

125 g (4½ oz/1 cup) plain (all-purpose) flour

175 g (6 oz/1 cup) rice flour

1 teaspoon baking powder

1 teaspoon mixed (pumpkin pie) spice

185 g (6½ oz/¾ cup) caster (superfine) sugar, plus extra to sprinkle

125 g (4½ oz) unsalted butter, melted

170 ml (5½ fl oz/⅔ cup) milk

2 eggs, lightly beaten

1 egg white, lightly beaten

1 Preheat the oven to 180°C (350°F/Gas 4). Lightly grease a 28 x 18 cm (11¼ x 7 inch) shallow baking tin and line with baking paper, making sure the paper overhangs two opposite sides. Soak the currants in the brandy, covered, for 15 minutes.

2 Sift the flours, baking powder and mixed spice into a large bowl. Stir in the sugar. Make a well in the centre, add the melted butter, milk and egg. Add the currants and mix gently.

3 Spoon the mixture evenly into the tin and smooth the surface. Brush with the egg white and sprinkle with sugar. Bake for 25 minutes, or until a skewer inserted into the slice comes out clean. Leave to cool in the tin, then lift out. Sprinkle again with sugar, then cut into pieces and serve.

STORAGE: *Store in an airtight container for up to 3 days.*

Sift the flours, baking powder and mixed spice into a large mixing bowl.

Make a well in the centre and add the melted butter, milk and egg.

Smooth the surface, then brush lightly with the beaten egg white.

Fruity chews

PREPARATION TIME: 30 MINUTES + COOLING | TOTAL COOKING TIME: 25 MINUTES | MAKES 16 PIECES

2 eggs
230 g (8½ oz/1 cup) firmly packed soft brown
    sugar
90 g (3¼ oz) unsalted butter, melted
1 teaspoon vanilla essence
185 g (6½ oz/1½ cups) plain (all-purpose) flour
1 teaspoon baking powder
140 g (5 oz/¾ cup) chopped dates
90 g (3¼ oz/¾ cup) chopped walnuts or pecans
110 g (3¾ oz/½ cup) chopped glacé (candied)
    ginger
50 g (1¾ oz/½ cup) rolled (porridge) oats

LEMON ICING
60 g (2¼ oz) unsalted butter
1 teaspoon grated lemon zest
125 g (4½ oz/1 cup) icing (confectioners') sugar
2 teaspoons lemon juice
75 g (2½ oz/⅓ cup) finely chopped glacé
    (candied) ginger

1 Preheat the oven to 180°C (350°F/Gas 4).
Lightly grease a 28 x 18 cm (11¼ x 7 inch)
shallow baking tin and line with baking paper,
making sure the paper overhangs on two
opposite sides.

2 Using electric beaters, beat the eggs and
brown sugar in a large mixing bowl for 1 minute,
or until well combined. Stir in the melted butter
and vanilla. Sift the flour and baking powder and
fold into the mixture with a metal spoon until
just combined. Do not overmix.

3 Stir in the remaining ingredients until well
combined. Spread into the prepared tin and
smooth the surface. Bake for 25 minutes, or
until lightly browned. Leave to cool in the tin.

4 To make the lemon icing (frosting), place the
butter and lemon zest in a small bowl and beat
with electric beaters until creamy. Gradually
add the sifted icing sugar, beating well after each
addition. Add enough lemon juice to make a
spreadable icing. Spread the lemon icing over the
cold slice, sprinkle with the ginger and cut into
pieces to serve.

Beat the eggs and brown sugar with electric
beaters for 1 minute.

Fold the flour and baking powder into the mixture
with a metal spoon.

Brandy mocha bars

PREPARATION TIME: 45 MINUTES + OVERNIGHT REFRIGERATION | TOTAL COOKING TIME: 15 MINUTES | MAKES 15 PIECES

1 tablespoon instant coffee
1 tablespoon boiling water
280 g (10 oz/2¼ cups) icing (confectioners') sugar
110 g (3¾ oz/1 cup) full-cream milk powder
60 g (2¼ oz/½ cup) unsweetened cocoa powder
2 eggs
3 tablespoons brandy
375 g (13 oz) white vegetable shortening, melted
125 g (4½ oz/1¼ cups) flaked almonds, toasted

BASE
125 g (4½ oz) unsalted butter
60 g (2¼ oz/¼ cup) caster (superfine) sugar
155 g (5½ oz/1¼ cups) plain (all-purpose) flour

CHOCOLATE ICING
250 g (9 oz/1⅔ cups) dark chocolate chopped
50 g (1¾ oz) white vegetable shortening, chopped
toasted flaked almonds, to decorate

1 Preheat the oven to 180°C (350°F/Gas 4). Lightly grease a shallow 23 cm (9 inch) square tin and line with baking paper, making sure the paper overhangs two opposite sides.

2 To make the base, beat the butter and sugar in a mixing bowl until just combined. Stir in the flour, then press into the prepared tin. Bake for 10 minutes, or until lightly browned. Cool.

3 Dissolve the coffee in water. Using electric beaters, beat the icing sugar, milk powder, cocoa, coffee, eggs and brandy until well combined. Gradually add the shortening and mix until well combined. Stir in the almonds then pour the mixture over the base. Refrigerate overnight, or until the topping is firm. Cut into small pieces.

4 To make the chocolate icing (frosting), place the chocolate and shortening in a heatproof bowl. Place the bowl over a saucepan of barely simmering water, making sure the base does not touch the water, and stir until the chocolate has melted. Dip the bars into the icing until coated and place on a wire rack over baking paper. Leave to set. Decorate with toasted flaked almonds.

Stir in the almonds, then pour the mixture over the cooled base.

Dip the bars into the chocolate icing, making sure they are completely coated.

Streuselkuchen slice

PREPARATION TIME: 40 MINUTES + 2 HOURS STANDING | TOTAL COOKING TIME: 45 MINUTES | MAKES 24 PIECES

2 teaspoons dried yeast

2 tablespoons lukewarm water

125 ml (4 fl oz/½ cup) milk

60 g (2¼ oz/¼ cup) caster (superfine) sugar

50 g (1¾ oz) unsalted butter

340 g (11¾ oz/2¾ cups) plain (all-purpose) flour

½ teaspoon salt

1 egg, lightly beaten

160 g (5¾ oz/½ cup) apricot jam

2 tablespoons water or lemon juice

2 x 410 g (14½ oz) tinned pie apples

CRUMBLE TOPPING

95 g (3¼ oz/½ cup) lightly packed soft brown sugar

40 g (1½ oz/⅓ cup) plain (all-purpose) flour

1 teaspoon ground cinnamon

60 g (2¼ oz) unsalted butter, cubed

125 g (4½ oz/1 cup) walnuts, roughly chopped

1 Lightly grease a 30 x 25 cm (12 x 10 inch) Swiss roll (jelly roll) tin. Dissolve the yeast in the warm water and set aside until frothy. Combine the milk, sugar and butter in a saucepan. Stir over medium heat until the butter has melted.

2 Sift 310 g (11 oz/2½ cups) of the flour and the salt into a large mixing bowl. Make a well in the centre and add the yeast and milk mixture and egg. Beat until well combined. Add enough of the remaining flour to form a soft dough. Turn onto a lightly floured surface and knead until smooth and elastic. Place dough in a lightly oiled bowl. Cover with lightly oiled plastic wrap and leave in a warm place for 1 hour or until well risen. Knead again for 1 minute. Divide in two, making one portion larger than the other. Roll out the larger portion to fit into the prepared tin. Place in the tin, pressing up the sides of the tin.

3 Combine the jam and water in a small pan and stir over low heat until the jam is slightly liquefied. Spread half over the dough. Top with the pie apple and remaining jam. Roll out the remaining dough to make a lid and place on the apple mixture. Scatter the crumble topping (see Step 4) thickly on top. Cover and leave in a warm place for about 1 hour or until well risen. Preheat the oven to 210°C (415°F/Gas 6–7). Bake for 5 minutes. Reduce the oven to 180°C (350°F/Gas 4), and bake for 30–40 minutes, or until the dough is cooked and the top is golden.

4 To make the crumble topping, combine the sugar, flour and cinnamon. Using fingertips, rub the butter in until the mixture resembles coarse breadcrumbs. Stir in the walnuts.

Dissolve the yeast in warm water and set aside for 5 minutes, or until frothy.

Knead the dough on a lightly floured surface for 10 minutes, or until smooth and elastic.

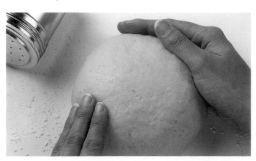

Fit the dough into the Swiss roll tin, carefully moulding it so it reaches up the sides.

Wholemeal lemon and walnut slice

PREPARATION TIME: 30 MINUTES | TOTAL COOKING TIME: 25 MINUTES | MAKES 16 PIECES

2 teaspoons finely grated lemon zest
40 g (1½ oz/⅓ cup) icing (confectioners') sugar
110 g (3¾ oz/¾ cup) wholemeal (whole-wheat) flour
30 g (1 oz/¼ cup) plain (all-purpose) flour
125 g (4½ oz/½ cup) raw (demerara) sugar
150 g (5½ oz/1¼ cups) walnuts, roughly chopped
90 g (3¼ oz/½ cup) mixed peel (mixed candied citrus peel), finely chopped
115 g (4 oz/⅓ cup) golden syrup (if unavailable, substitute with half honey and half dark corn syrup)
125 g (4½ oz) unsalted butter, chopped

1 Put the lemon zest and icing sugar in a small bowl and rub gently to just combine. Spread out on a plate and leave to dry.

2 Preheat the oven to 180°C (350°F/Gas 4). Lightly grease a 27 x 18 cm (10¾ x 7 inch) shallow baking tin and line with baking paper, making sure the paper overhangs on two opposite sides.

3 Sift the flours into a large mixing bowl, returning any husks to the bowl. Stir in the raw sugar, walnuts and mixed peel.

4 Put the syrup and butter in a saucepan and stir over low heat until melted. Add to the bowl and mix well. Spread into the prepared tin and bake for 20–25 minutes, or until golden brown and a skewer inserted into the centre comes out clean. Leave to cool completely in the tin. Put the lemon sugar in a sieve and sprinkle over the slice before cutting into fingers or squares.

Rub the lemon zest and icing sugar between your fingertips to flavour the sugar.

Sift the flours into a bowl, returning any husks from the wholemeal flour to the bowl.

Press the mixture into the prepared tin with a spoon and bake for 20–25 minutes.

Brandy Alexander slice

PREPARATION TIME: 20 MINUTES + OVERNIGHT REFRIGERATION | TOTAL COOKING TIME: 5 MINUTES | MAKES 12 PIECES

80 g (2¾ oz) unsalted butter, chopped

60 g (2¼ oz) dark cooking chocolate, chopped

250 g (9 oz) packet plain chocolate biscuits, finely crushed

300 g (10½ oz) ricotta cheese

60 ml (2 fl oz/¼ cup) cream

40 g (1½ oz/⅓ cup) icing (confectioners') sugar, sifted

60 g (2¼ oz/½ cup) grated milk chocolate

1 tablespoon brandy

1 tablespoon crème de cacao liqueur (see VARIATION)

½ teaspoon ground nutmeg

60 g (2¼ oz) dark chocolate melts (buttons)

1 Lightly grease a shallow 30 x 20 cm (12 x 8 inch) rectangular baking tin and line with baking paper. Place the butter and dark chocolate in a small heatproof bowl. Stand over a saucepan of simmering water and stir until the chocolate is melted and the mixture is smooth. Remove from the heat. Using a flat-bladed knife, mix the chocolate mixture with the biscuit crumbs in a small mixing bowl.

2 Press the biscuit mixture evenly over the base of the prepared tin and set aside.

3 Using electric beaters, beat the ricotta, cream and icing sugar in a small mixing bowl on medium speed for 3 minutes, or until the mixture is light and creamy. Add the grated chocolate, brandy and liqueur and beat until combined.

4 Spread the cheese mixture over the prepared base and sprinkle with the nutmeg. Refrigerate for several hours or overnight. Cut into 12 pieces. Place the chocolate melts in a small heatproof bowl and stand over simmering water until melted. Place in a small piping (icing) bag and pipe a design on top of each bar.

STORAGE: *Store in the refrigerator for up to 2 days.*

VARIATION: *Use Tia Maria in place of the crème de cacao.*

Press the biscuit mixture firmly into the prepared baking tin, making sure it is evenly distributed.

Add the chocolate, brandy and liqueur to the light and creamy mixture.

Chocolate hedgehog slice

PREPARATION TIME: 30 MINUTES I TOTAL COOKING TIME: 5–10 MINUTES + 30 MINUTES REFRIGERATION I MAKES 40 PIECES

250 g (9 oz) chocolate cream biscuits, finely crushed

45 g (1½ oz/½ cup) desiccated coconut

125 g (4½ oz) chopped pecans

1 tablespoon unsweetened cocoa powder, sifted

100 g (3½ oz) dark chocolate, chopped

80 g (2¾ oz) unsalted butter

1 tablespoon golden syrup (if unavailable, substitute with half honey and half dark corn syrup)

1 egg, lightly beaten

60 g (2¼ oz) dark chocolate melts (buttons), extra

extra pecans, for decoration

ICING

100 g (3½ oz) dark chocolate, chopped

40 g (1½ oz) unsalted butter

1 Line the base and sides of a shallow 30 x 20 cm (12 x 8 inch) rectangular baking tin with foil. Combine the biscuit crumbs, coconut, pecans and cocoa in a medium mixing bowl. Make a well in the centre of the ingredients.

2 Combine the chocolate, butter and syrup in a small heavy-based saucepan. Stir over low heat until the chocolate and butter have melted and the mixture is smooth. Remove from the heat. Pour the chocolate mixture and egg into the dry ingredients. Using a wooden spoon, stir until well combined. Press the mixture evenly into the prepared tin. Refrigerate for 30 minutes, or until set.

3 Place the extra dark chocolate in a small heatproof bowl and stand over simmering water until melted. Dip one half of each pecans in the chocolate and leave to set.

4 To make the icing (frosting), place the chocolate and butter in a small heatproof bowl. Stand over a saucepan of simmering water, making sure the base does not touch the water. Stir until the chocolate and butter have melted and the mixture is smooth. Cool slightly. Spread the mixture evenly over the slice base and refrigerate until set. Remove from the tin and cut into small squares. Decorate with the dipped pecans.

Combine the ingredients with a wooden spoon, making a well in the centre.

Add the chocolate mixture and the lightly beaten egg and stir with a wooden spoon.

After the slice has set, place a chocolate-dipped pecan on top of each square.

Berry almond slice

PREPARATION TIME: 25 MINUTES | TOTAL COOKING TIME: 1 HOUR 5 MINUTES | MAKES 15 PIECES

1 sheet frozen puff pastry, thawed
150 g (5½ oz) unsalted butter
185 g (6½ oz/¾ cup) caster (superfine) sugar
3 eggs, lightly beaten
2 tablespoons grated lemon zest
125 g (4½ oz/1¼ cups) ground almonds
2 tablespoons plain (all-purpose) flour
150 g (5½ oz) fresh raspberries
150 g (5½ oz) fresh blackberries
icing (confectioners') sugar, to dust

1   Preheat the oven to 200°C (400°F/Gas 6). Lightly grease a 23 cm (9 inch) square shallow baking tin and line with baking paper, making sure the paper overhangs on two opposite sides.

2   Place the pastry on a baking tray lined with baking paper. Prick all over with a fork and bake for 15 minutes, or until golden. Ease the pastry into the tin, trimming the edges if necessary. Reduce the oven to 180°C (350°F/Gas 4).

3   Using electric beaters, beat the butter and sugar in a mixing bowl until light and fluffy. Add the egg, a little at a time, beating after every addition, then add the lemon zest. Fold in the ground almonds and flour. Spread the mixture over the pastry base. Scatter the fruit on top and bake for 45–50 minutes, or until lightly golden. Cool in the tin before lifting out to cut. Dust with icing sugar and serve.

Ease the cooked pastry into the lined tin, trimming the edges if necessary.

Fold the ground almonds and flour into the beaten mixture and spread over the base.

Frozen berries can be used instead; simply make sure they are thawed and drained.

Peach crumble slice

PREPARATION TIME: 30 MINUTES | TOTAL COOKING TIME: 1 HOUR | MAKES 9 PIECES

60 g (2¼ oz/½ cup) self-raising flour
90 g (3¼ oz/¾ cup) plain (all-purpose) flour
60 g (2¼ oz/1 cup) shredded coconut
50 g (1¾ oz/½ cup) rolled (porridge) oats
95 g (3¼ oz/½ cup) lightly packed soft brown sugar
160 g (5¾ oz) unsalted butter, melted
1 teaspoon vanilla essence
2 x 415 g (14¾ oz) tinned pie peaches
2 tablespoons honey
60 g (2¼ oz/½ cup) sultanas (golden raisins)
¼ teaspoon ground cinnamon

1 Preheat the oven to 180°C (350°F/Gas 4). Lightly grease a 28 x 18 cm (11¼ x 7 inch) shallow baking tin and line with baking paper, making sure the paper overhangs on two opposite sides.

2 Sift the flours into a mixing bowl. Stir in the coconut, rolled oats and brown sugar. Mix in the butter and vanilla.

3 Set aside a third of the mixture and press the rest into the prepared tin. Smooth the surface and bake for 15–20 minutes. Leave to cool in the tin.

4 Mix the peaches, honey and sultanas in a bowl and spread over the base. Mix the cinnamon into the reserved crumble mixture and sprinkle over the top. Bake for 35–40 minutes, or until golden. Leave to cool, then cut into pieces to serve.

Press the crumbly base into the tin, smoothing the surface with the back of a spoon.

Mix together the peaches, honey and sultanas and spread over the base.

Sprinkle the remaining crumble mixture over the top and bake until golden.

Vanilla and passionfruit slice

PREPARATION TIME: 35 MINUTES + 2 HOURS REFRIGERATION | TOTAL COOKING TIME: 20–25 MINUTES | MAKES 12 PIECES

2 sheets frozen puff pastry, thawed

CUSTARD
30 g (1 oz/¼ cup) custard powder
60 g (2¼ oz/¼ cup) caster (superfine) sugar
250 ml (9 fl oz/1 cup) cream
375 ml (13 fl oz/1½ cups) milk
½ teaspoon vanilla essence

ICING
60 g (2¼ oz/¼ cup) passionfruit pulp
25 g (1 oz) unsalted butter
185 g (6½ oz/1½ cups) icing (confectioners')
  sugar

1 Preheat the oven to 210°C (415°F/Gas 6–7). Line two baking trays with baking paper. Place the puff pastry sheets on the prepared trays and prick all over with a fork. Bake for 10–15 minutes, or until golden and crisp. Cool on a wire rack.

2 To make the custard, combine the custard powder, sugar and cream in a medium-sized heavy-based saucepan. Gradually stir in the milk and stir constantly over medium heat until the custard boils and thickens. Remove from the heat. Stir in the vanilla. Place plastic wrap onto the surface of the custard to prevent a skin forming. Cool.

3 Place one sheet of pastry onto a board. Spread the custard evenly over the surface. Top with the remaining pastry sheet upside down.

4 To make the icing (frosting), combine the passionfruit pulp, butter and icing sugar in a medium heatproof bowl. Stand over a saucepan of simmering water and stir until the icing is smooth and glossy. Remove from the heat. Spread the icing evenly over the pastry sheet, using a flat-bladed knife. Refrigerate for several hours or until the pastry softens slightly. Cut the slice into 12 squares using a serrated knife.

STORAGE: *Store in an airtight container in the refrigerator for up to 2 days.*

Prick the pastry sheets with a fork before baking for 10–15 minutes, or until golden.

Spread the first sheet of puff pastry with custard, then top with the other.

Finish the slice off with a layer of passionfruit icing before chilling for several hours.

Choc-caramel slice

PREPARATION TIME: 40 MINUTES + REFRIGERATION | TOTAL COOKING TIME: 30 MINUTES | MAKES 24 TRIANGLES

125 g (4½ oz) plain sweet biscuits, crushed
80 g (2¾ oz) unsalted butter, melted
2 tablespoons desiccated coconut
400 g (14 oz) tin sweetened condensed milk
125 g (4½ oz) unsalted butter
90 g (3¼ oz/⅓ cup) caster (superfine) sugar
115 g (4 oz/⅓ cup) golden syrup (if unavailable, substitute with half honey and half dark corn syrup)
250 g (9 oz/1⅔ cups) chocolate melts (buttons)
1 tablespoon vegetable oil

1 Lightly grease a shallow 30 x 20 cm (12 x 8 inch) rectangular baking tin and line with foil. Grease the foil. Combine the crushed biscuits, butter and coconut in a medium-sized mixing bowl. Press the mixture evenly into the prepared tin and smooth the surface.

2 Combine the condensed milk, butter, sugar and golden syrup in a small saucepan. Stir over low heat for 25 minutes or until the sugar has dissolved and the mixture is smooth, thick and lightly browned. Remove from the heat and leave to cool slightly. Pour over the biscuit base and smooth the surface.

3 Place the milk chocolate melts and oil in a small heatproof bowl. Stand over a saucepan of simmering water, stir until melted. Spread the chocolate mixture over the caramel. Allow to partially set before marking into 24 triangles. Refrigerate until firm, then cut into triangles.

STORAGE: *The slice may be stored in an airtight container for up to 2 days.*

Press the biscuit mixture firmly into the prepared tin, making sure it is evenly spread.

To make the caramel, heat the condensed milk, butter, sugar and golden syrup until thick.

Using a sharp knife, mark the 24 triangles before chilling and then cutting.

Cappuccino slice

PREPARATION TIME: 30 MINUTES + COOLING | TOTAL COOKING TIME: 55 MINUTES | MAKES 16 PIECES

40 g (1½ oz/⅓ cup) self-raising flour
30 g (1 oz/¼ cup) plain (all-purpose) flour
1 tablespoon unsweetened cocoa powder
60 g (2¼ oz/¼ cup) caster (superfine) sugar
1 egg, lightly beaten
1 teaspoon vanilla essence
65 g (2¼ oz) unsalted butter, melted
60 ml (2 fl oz/¼ cup) milk

CAPPUCCINO FILLING
350 g (12 oz) cream cheese
100 g (3½ oz) mascarpone cheese
90 g (3¼ oz/⅓ cup) sour cream
90 g (3¼ oz/⅓ cup) caster (superfine) sugar
3 eggs, lightly beaten
1 tablespoon instant coffee
1 tablespoon warm water
50 g (1¾ oz) dark chocolate, grated

1 Preheat the oven to 180°C (350°F/Gas 4). Lightly grease a 19 cm (7½ inch) square cake tin and line with baking paper, making sure the paper overhangs on two opposite sides.

2 Sift the flours and cocoa into a large mixing bowl. Add the sugar and make a well in the centre of the dry ingredients. In a separate bowl, mix the egg, vanilla, butter and milk until well combined. Pour the egg mixture into the dry ingredients and stir until just combined. Spoon into the prepared tin and bake for 10–15 minutes and then cool completely. Reduce the oven to 160°C (315°F/Gas 2–3).

3 To make the filling, beat the cream cheese, mascarpone and sour cream with electric beaters for 3 minutes, or until smooth. Add the sugar in batches and beat for another 3 minutes. Add the eggs gradually, beating well after each addition.

4 Dissolve the coffee in a little warm water, add to the filling and beat until well combined. Pour over the base. Bake for 40 minutes, or until set. Leave in the tin to cool completely. Cut into slices, top with grated chocolate and serve.

Stir the egg, vanilla, butter and milk into the dry ingredients until well combined.

Pour the filling mixture over the base and bake for 40 minutes.

Apple custard streusel slice

PREPARATION TIME: 30 MINUTES + 20 MINUTES REFRIGERATION | TOTAL COOKING TIME: 1 HOUR | MAKES 15 PIECES

PASTRY
155 g (5½ oz/1¼ cups) plain (all-purpose) flour
1 tablespoon caster (superfine) sugar
80 g (2¾ oz) unsalted butter, melted and cooled
1 egg yolk

APPLE CUSTARD TOPPING
3 green apples, peeled, cored and chopped
20 g (¾ oz) unsalted butter
4 tablespoons caster (superfine) sugar
2 eggs
185 ml (6 fl oz/¾ cup) whipping cream
1 teaspoon vanilla essence

CRUMBLE TOPPING
60 g (2¼ oz/½ cup) plain (all-purpose) flour
2 tablespoons dark brown sugar
40 g (1½ oz/⅓ cup) finely chopped walnuts
60 g (2¼ oz) unsalted butter, melted

1 Lightly grease a 28 x 18 cm (11¼ x 7 inch) shallow baking tin and line with baking paper, making sure the paper overhangs on two opposite sides.

2 To make the pastry, sift the flour and sugar into a bowl. Add the butter, egg yolk and 2–3 tablespoons water and mix until the dough comes together. Roll out between two sheets of baking paper to fit the base of the tin. Refrigerate for 20 minutes. Preheat the oven to 190°C (375°F/Gas 5).

3 Line the pastry base with baking paper and fill with baking beads, or uncooked rice. Bake for 15 minutes. Remove the paper and beads, reduce oven to 180°C (350°F/Gas 4) and bake for 5 minutes, or until golden. Leave to cool.

4 To make the apple custard topping, place the apple in a saucepan with the butter, half the sugar and 2 tablespoons water. Cover and cook over low heat until soft. Uncover and simmer for 5 minutes to reduce the liquid. Use a wooden spoon to break down the apples until smooth. Cool. Whisk together the eggs, cream, remaining sugar and vanilla. Spread the apple mixture over the base, then pour over the cream mixture. Bake for 20 minutes, or until the custard has half set.

5 To make the crumble topping, mix together the flour, brown sugar and walnuts in a mixing bowl. Stir in the melted butter until mixture is crumbly. Sprinkle over the custard and bake for 15 minutes. Cool in the tin before slicing.

Roll out the pastry between two sheets of baking paper until big enough to fit the tin's base.

Bake for 15 minutes, then remove the paper and baking beads or uncooked rice.

Sprinkle the crumble topping over the custard and bake for 15 minutes.

Lemon and almond slice

PREPARATION TIME: 25 MINUTES I TOTAL COOKING TIME: 1 HOUR I MAKES 18 PIECES

60 g (2¼ oz/½ cup) plain (all-purpose) flour
40 g (1½ oz/⅓ cup) self-raising flour
2 tablespoons icing (confectioners') sugar
60 g (2¼ oz) unsalted butter, chopped
1 egg, lightly beaten
whipped cream, to serve
lemon zest, to garnish

ALMOND CREAM

3 eggs, at room temperature
125 g (4½ oz/½ cup) caster (superfine) sugar
2 teaspoons grated lemon zest
125 ml (4 fl oz/½ cup) lemon juice
80 g (2¾ oz/¾ cup) ground almonds
250 ml (9 fl oz/1 cup) cream

1 Preheat the oven to 190°C (375°F/Gas 5). Lightly grease a 23 cm (9 inch) square shallow baking tin.

2 Put the flours, sugar and butter in a food processor and process until the mixture resembles fine breadcrumbs. Add the egg and process briefly, until the dough just comes together, adding a small amount of water if necessary.

3 Press the dough into the base of the prepared tin and prick well with a fork. Bake for 10–12 minutes, or until golden. Allow to cool. Reduce the oven to 170°C (325°F/Gas 3).

4 To make the almond cream, beat the eggs and sugar with a wooden spoon. Stir in the lemon zest, lemon juice, ground almonds and cream. Pour over the pastry and bake for 35–40 minutes, or until lightly set. Leave to cool in the tin. Slice into pieces and garnish with lemon zest. Serve with whipped cream.

Press the dough into the tin and prick all over with a fork before baking.

Beat the eggs and sugar, then stir in the zest, juice, ground almonds and cream.

Plum and almond slice

PREPARATION TIME: 30 MINUTES | TOTAL COOKING TIME: 1 HOUR 10 MINUTES | MAKES 9 PIECES

160 g (5½ oz) unsalted butter
160 g (5½ oz/⅔ cup) caster (superfine) sugar
2 eggs
60 g (2¼ oz/½ cup) plain (all-purpose) flour
40 g (1½ oz/⅓ cup) cornflour (cornstarch)
2 tablespoons rice flour
1½ tablespoons thinly sliced glacé (candied)
    ginger
825 g (1 lb 13 oz) tinned plums in syrup,
    drained and halved (see NOTE)
100 g (3½ oz/1 cup) flaked almonds
1 tablespoon warmed honey

1   Preheat the oven to 180°C (350°F/Gas 4).
Lightly grease a 20 cm (8 inch) square baking tin
and line with baking paper, extending over the
top edge of the tin on all sides.

2   Using electric beaters, beat the butter and
sugar in a mixing bowl until light and creamy.
Add the eggs one at a time, beating well after
each addition. Fold the sifted flours into the
mixture with the ginger. Spread into the tin.
Arrange the plums on top, pressing them in.
Scatter with the almonds, pressing in gently, then
drizzle with the honey.

3   Bake for 1 hour 10 minutes, or until firm and
golden (cover with foil if slice is over-browning).
Cool before cutting.

NOTE: *If in season, use 7 ripe blood plums
instead of tinned. They might bleed more than
the tinned variety.*

Drain the tinned plums and cut in half, carefully removing the stones.

Arrange the plum halves on top, pressing them gently into the filling mixture.

Scatter the flaked almonds over the top, then drizzle with the honey.

Ginger and macadamia squares

PREPARATION TIME: 20 MINUTES | TOTAL COOKING TIME: 35 MINUTES | MAKES 20 SQUARES

125 g (4½ oz) unsalted butter
185 g (6½ oz/1 cup) lightly packed soft
    brown sugar
2 eggs, lightly beaten
175 g (6 oz/1¼ cups) self-raising flour
4 teaspoons ground ginger

WHITE CHOCOLATE ICING
150 g (5½ oz) white chocolate, chopped
60 ml (2 fl oz/¼ cup) cream
2 tablespoons chopped glacé (candied)
    ginger
2 tablespoons chopped macadamia nuts
    (see VARIATION)

1 Preheat the oven to 180°C (350°F/Gas 4).
Grease a shallow 27 x 18 cm (10¾ x 7 inch)
rectangular baking tin. Cover the base with
baking paper, making sure the paper overhangs
on two opposite sides, and grease the paper.

2 Using electric beaters, beat the butter and
sugar in a small mixing bowl until light and
creamy. Add the eggs a little at a time, beating
thoroughly after each addition. Transfer the
mixture to a large mixing bowl. Using a metal
spoon, fold in the sifted flour and ginger
and stir until just combined.

3 Spread the mixture into the prepared tin.
Bake for 30 minutes, or until golden and firm
in the centre. Leave to cool in the tin.

4 To make the white chocolate icing
(frosting), combine the chocolate and cream
in a small saucepan. Stir over low heat until
the chocolate has melted and the mixture is
smooth. Leave to cool. Using a flat-bladed
knife, spread the icing evenly over the slice.
Sprinkle with the glacé ginger and macadamia
nuts. Allow the icing to set and then cut into
squares to serve.

STORAGE: *Store for up to 3 days in an airtight
container or up to 2 months in the freezer
un-iced.*

VARIATION: *Any chopped nuts, such as
walnuts, pecans or toasted almonds are suitable
for this recipe.*

Place the mixture into the prepared tin and spread
evenly with a spatula.

While the slice is still in the tin, spread the icing
over the top with a flat-bladed knife.

Caramel pecan squares

PREPARATION TIME: 25 MINUTES + 3 HOURS REFRIGERATION | TOTAL COOKING TIME: 35 MINUTES | MAKES 16 PIECES

250 g (9 oz) plain chocolate biscuits
1 tablespoon drinking chocolate
150 g (5½ oz/1½ cups) pecans
110 g (3¾ oz) unsalted butter, melted

CARAMEL TOPPING
90 g (3¼ oz/½ cup) lightly packed soft brown
    sugar
60 g (2¼ oz) unsalted butter
400 g (14 oz) tin sweetened condensed milk
icing (confectioners') sugar, to dust
drinking chocolate, to dust

1   Preheat the oven to 180°C (350°F/Gas 4).
Lightly grease a 28 x 18 cm (11¼ x 7 inch)
shallow baking tin and line with baking paper,
making sure the paper overhangs on two
opposite sides.

2   Finely crush the biscuits, drinking chocolate
and a third of the pecans in a food processor.
Transfer to a mixing bowl and add the melted
butter. Mix well and press firmly into the
prepared tin. Press the rest of the pecans gently
over the top.

3   To make the caramel topping, place the
brown sugar and butter in a saucepan over low
heat. Stir until the butter melts and the sugar
dissolves. Add the condensed milk and cook,
stirring, until thicker and slightly darker. Pour
over the biscuit base.

4   Bake for 25–30 minutes, or until the caramel
is firm and golden—the edges will bubble and
darken. Cool, then refrigerate for at least 3 hours.
Trim off the crusty edges and cut the slice into
squares. Before serving, hold a piece of paper
over one half of each piece and sprinkle the other
half with icing sugar. Sprinkle the other side with
drinking chocolate.

Arrange the rest of the pecans over the base,
pressing them in gently.

Trim the crusty edges off the slice before cutting
into squares to serve.

Walnut brownies

PREPARATION TIME: 20 MINUTES | TOTAL COOKING TIME: 35 MINUTES | MAKES 20 DIAMONDS

100 g (3½ oz) unsalted butter
125 g (4½ oz/⅔ cup) lightly packed soft brown
    sugar
40 g (1½ oz/⅓ cup) sultanas (golden raisins),
    chopped
125 g (4½ oz/1 cup) self-raising flour
125 g (4½ oz/1 cup) plain (all-purpose) flour
1 teaspoon ground cinnamon
1 tablespoon unsweetened cocoa powder
60 g (2¼ oz/½ cup) chopped walnuts
90 g (3¼ oz) chocolate chips
20 walnut halves

ICING
60 g (2¼ oz) unsalted butter
90 g (3¼ oz/¾ cup) icing (confectioners') sugar
1 tablespoon unsweetened cocoa powder
1 tablespoon milk

1 Preheat the oven to 180°C (350°F/Gas 4). Lightly grease a 27 x 18 cm (10¾ x 7 inch) shallow rectangular baking tin. Line the base with baking paper, extending it over the two longer sides. Grease the paper. Combine butter, sugar, sultanas and 185 ml (6 fl oz/¾ cup) water in a small saucepan. Constantly stir over low heat for 5 minutes, or until the butter is melted and the sugar is dissolved. Remove from the heat.

2 Sift the dry ingredients into a large mixing bowl and add the chopped nuts and chocolate chips. Make a well in the centre of the dry ingredients and add the butter mixture. Using a wooden spoon, stir until just combined. Do not overmix.

3 Spoon the mixture into the prepared tin and smooth the surface. Bake for 25–30 minutes, or until a skewer comes out clean when inserted in the centre of the slice. Leave in the tin for 20 minutes before turning onto a wire rack to cool completely.

4 To make the icing (frosting), beat the butter with electric beaters until light and creamy. Add the icing sugar, cocoa and milk. Beat until smooth. Spread the icing over the brownie. Cut into diamonds and top with the walnut halves.

Bake for 25–30 minutes and test to see if the brownie base is cooked by inserting a skewer in the centre.

Spread the icing over the top then slice into diamonds with a sharp knife.

Frangipane slice

PREPARATION TIME: 40 MINUTES I TOTAL COOKING TIME: 50 MINUTES I MAKES 15 PIECES

90 g (3¼ oz) unsalted butter
90 g (3¼ oz/⅓ cup) caster (superfine) sugar
1 teaspoon vanilla essence
1 egg, lightly beaten
90 g (3¼ oz/⅔ cup) plain (all-purpose) flour
40 g (1½ oz/⅓ cup) self-raising flour

ALMOND FILLING
90 g (3¼ oz) unsalted butter
90 g (3¼ oz/⅓ cup) caster (superfine) sugar
2 eggs, lightly beaten
180 g (6½ oz/1¾ cups) ground almonds
30 g (1 oz/¼ cup) plain (all-purpose) flour

ALMOND TOPPING
60 g (2¼ oz) unsalted butter
60 g (2¼ oz/¼ cup) caster (superfine) sugar
1 tablespoon honey
60 g (2¼ oz/⅔ cup) flaked almonds

1 Preheat the oven to 180°C (350°F/Gas 4). Lightly grease a 28 x 18 cm (11¼ x 7 inch) shallow baking tin and line with baking paper, making sure the paper overhangs on two opposite sides.

2 Using electric beaters, beat the butter, sugar and vanilla in a mixing bowl until light and creamy. Add the egg and beat well.

3 Sift the flours together and fold into the mixture with a metal spoon. Spread evenly into the prepared tin.

4 To make the almond filling, beat the butter and sugar with electric beaters until light and creamy. Beat in the egg, a little at a time—the mixture will look curdled—mixing well after each addition. Stir in the ground almonds and flour then spread over the base. Bake for 25–30 minutes, or until firm and golden. Leave in the tin to cool.

5 Put the almond topping ingredients in a small saucepan. Bring slowly to the boil, stirring to dissolve the sugar. Boil gently for 2 minutes, or until the mixture starts to come away from the side of the saucepan. Quickly spread over the slice with a metal spatula. Bake for 10–15 minutes, or until golden brown, taking care not to burn the topping. Cool in the tin, then lift out and cut into pieces to serve.

Stir the ground almonds and flour into the filling mixture until well combined.

Boil the almond topping gently until it starts to come away from the side of the saucepan.

Lime custard slice

PREPARATION TIME: 30 MINUTES + 3 HOURS REFRIGERATION | TOTAL COOKING TIME: 10 MINUTES | MAKES 12 PIECES

250 g (9 oz) plain sweet biscuits, crushed
120 g (4¼ oz) unsalted butter, melted
40 g (1½ oz/⅓ cup) custard powder
250 g (9 oz/1 cup) caster (superfine) sugar
60 g (2¼ oz/½ cup) cornflour (cornstarch)
750 ml (26 fl oz/3 cups) milk
250 ml (9 fl oz/1 cup) lime juice
60 g (2¼ oz) unsalted butter
3 egg yolks
lime zest, cut into strips, to garnish

1 Lightly grease a 30 x 20 cm (12 x 8 inch) shallow baking tin and line with baking paper, making sure the paper overhangs on two sides.

2 Combine the biscuit crumbs and the 120 g (4¼ oz) of the melted butter and press firmly into the prepared tin and refrigerate.

3 Put the custard powder, sugar and cornflour in a saucepan. Mix the milk, lime juice and 185 ml (6 fl oz/¾ cup) water in a separate bowl and gradually stir into the custard mixture. Stir over medium heat for 5 minutes, or until the custard thickens. Remove and cool a little. Whisk in the 60 g (2¼ oz) of the butter and egg yolks.

4 Pour over the base and chill for 2–3 hours. Cut the slice into 12 pieces and garnish each piece with strips of lime zest.

Press the biscuit crumb base into the prepared tin, making sure it is evenly distributed.

Using a wooden spoon, stir the custard mixture over medium heat until it boils and thickens.

Remove the custard mixture from the heat, cool slightly and whisk in the butter and egg yolks.

Apple and cinnamon slice

PREPARATION TIME: 15 MINUTES | TOTAL COOKING TIME: 35 MINUTES | MAKES ABOUT 20 SLICES

125 g (4½ oz) unsalted butter
125 g (4½ oz/½ cup) caster (superfine) sugar
2 eggs
250 g (9 oz/2 cups) self-raising flour, sifted
300 g (10½ oz/1¼ cups) sour cream
2 green apples, peeled, cored and sliced
60 g (2¼ oz/½ cup) finely chopped pecans
2 tablespoons caster (superfine) sugar
1 teaspoon ground cinnamon

1 Preheat the oven to 180°C (350°F/Gas 4). Lightly grease a 30 x 20 cm (12 x 8 inch) shallow baking tin and line with baking paper, making sure the paper overhangs on two opposite sides. Using electric beaters, beat the butter and sugar until light and creamy. Add the eggs one at a time, beating well after each addition. Transfer to a large mixing bowl.

2 Using a metal spoon, fold in the flour. Add the sour cream and stir to combine. Spoon the mixture into the prepared tin.

3 Arrange the apples over the slice base. Sprinkle with the combined pecans, sugar and cinnamon. Bake for 30–35 minutes. Leave to cool in the tin. Cut into squares or rectangles to serve.

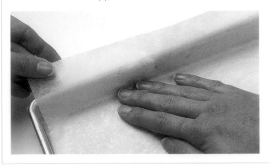
Line the cake tin with baking paper so that the paper extends over two opposite sides.

Add the sour cream to the mixture and stir until well combined.

Arrange the apples over the slice base and sprinkle with the pecan mixture.

Choc-raspberry cheesecake slice

PREPARATION TIME: 1 HOUR + OVERNIGHT REFRIGERATION | TOTAL COOKING TIME: 5 MINUTES | MAKES 16 PIECES

150 g (5½ oz) sweet biscuits, crushed
80 g (2¾ oz) unsalted butter, melted
½ teaspoon mixed (pumpkin pie) spice
1 tablespoon gelatine
100 g (3½ oz) white chocolate
125 g (4½ oz) cream cheese, softened
90 g (3¼ oz/⅓ cup) caster (superfine) sugar
1 egg
250 ml (9 fl oz/1 cup) cream
1 teaspoon vanilla essence
300 g (10½ oz) fresh or frozen raspberries
    (see NOTE)

1   Line a 20 cm (8 inch) square cake tin with baking paper, covering the base and overhanging on all sides.

2   Mix together the biscuit crumbs, melted butter and mixed spice and press evenly into the prepared tin. Refrigerate until set.

3   Dissolve the gelatine in 2 tablespoons water, then leave to cool slightly. Place the chocolate in a heatproof bowl and sit over a saucepan of barely simmering water, making sure the base of the bowl does not touch the water. Stir the chocolate until melted. Leave to cool.

4   Using electric beaters, beat the cream cheese and sugar in a mixing bowl until light and creamy. Beat in the egg, cream and vanilla until just combined. With the beaters running at low speed, add the cooled gelatine and melted chocolate to the mixture and mix until just combined. Do not overmix.

5   Pour the mixture over the set biscuit base, then scatter with the raspberries, gently pressing them down. Refrigerate overnight to set. Using a sharp knife dipped in hot water, cut the slice into small squares.

NOTE: *If you are using frozen raspberries, defrost and drain them well on paper towels before using.*

HINT: *Make sure the melted chocolate and gelatine have cooled before beating them into the cream cheese mixture or they'll become lumpy.*

Use the back of a spoon to firmly press the crumb base into the prepared tin.

Adjust the electric beaters to low speed when adding the gelatine and chocolate.

Scatter the raspberries over the chocolate cream cheese mixture, pressing them down a little.

Continental slice

PREPARATION TIME: 25 MINUTES + 4 HOURS REFRIGERATION | TOTAL COOKING TIME: 10 MINUTES | MAKES ABOUT 24 PIECES

125 g (4½ oz) unsalted butter
125 g (4½ oz/½ cup) caster (superfine) sugar
30 g (1 oz/¼ cup) unsweetened cocoa powder
250 g (9 oz) shredded wheat biscuits, crushed
75 g (2½ oz/¾ cup) desiccated coconut
30 g (1 oz/¼ cup) chopped hazelnuts
60 g (2¼ oz/¼ cup) chopped glacé (candied) cherries
1 egg, lightly beaten
1 teaspoon vanilla essence

TOPPING
60 g (2¼ oz) unsalted butter
220 g (7¾ oz/1¾ cups) icing (confectioners') sugar
2 tablespoons custard powder
1 tablespoon hot water
1 tablespoon Grand Marnier (orange liquor)
125 g (4½ oz) dark chocolate
60 g (2¼ oz) white vegetable shortening

1 Line the base and sides of a 28 x 18 cm (11¼ x 7 inch) shallow baking tin with foil. Combine the butter, sugar and cocoa in a small saucepan. Stir over low heat until the butter melts and the mixture is well combined. Cook, stirring, for 1 minute. Remove from the heat and cool slightly. Combine the biscuit crumbs, coconut, hazelnuts and cherries in a large mixing bowl. Make a well in the centre and add the butter mixture, egg and vanilla and stir well. Press the mixture firmly into the prepared tin. Refrigerate until firm.

2 To make the topping, beat the butter with electric beaters until creamy. Gradually add the icing sugar and custard powder, alternately with the hot water and Grand Marnier. Beat the mixture until light and fluffy. Spread evenly over the base. Refrigerate until set.

3 Place the chocolate and shortening in a heatproof bowl and set over a saucepan of simmering water. Stir over low heat until the chocolate melts and the mixture is smooth. Spread over the slice. Refrigerate until firm. Cut into small squares to serve.

Gradually add the icing sugar and custard powder to the creamed butter.

Spread the chocolate topping evenly over the chilled slice base.

Hazelnut truffle slice

PREPARATION TIME: 30 MINUTES + 2 HOURS REFRIGERATION | TOTAL COOKING TIME: 40 MINUTES | MAKES 24 PIECES

100 g (3½ oz) hazelnuts
80 g (2¾ oz) unsalted butter
90 g (3¼ oz/⅓ cup) caster (superfine) sugar
90 g (3¼ oz/¾ cup) plain (all-purpose) flour
1½ tablespoons unsweetened cocoa powder

CHOCOLATE BRANDY ICING
200 g (7 oz) dark chocolate, chopped
    (see NOTE)
125 ml (4 fl oz/½ cup) cream
2 teaspoons brandy or rum

1   Preheat the oven to 180°C (350°F/Gas 4). Lightly grease a 21 x 11 cm (8¼ x 4¼ inch) loaf (bar) tin and line with baking paper, making sure the paper overhangs on two opposite sides.

2   Spread the hazelnuts on a baking tray and bake for 7 minutes, or until lightly browned. Remove from the oven and, while they are still hot, wrap them in a tea towel (dish towel) and rub away the skins. Cool, then chop roughly.

3   Beat the butter and sugar with electric beaters until light and creamy. Sift the flour and cocoa powder into a bowl, then stir into the butter mixture. Press evenly over the base of the tin and bake for 25–30 minutes, or until firm. Leave to cool completely.

4   To make the chocolate brandy icing (frosting), place the chocolate and cream in a small saucepan. Stir over low heat until the chocolate has melted and the mixture is very smooth. Do not overheat. Leave the mixture to cool slightly, then add the brandy or rum and stir until well combined.

5   Stir the hazelnuts into the icing, then pour over the cooled pastry base. Refrigerate for several hours, or until the topping is firm. The slice is very rich, so cut into small pieces to serve.

STORAGE: *Store for up to 1 week in an airtight container. Store in the fridge in warm weather.*

NOTE: *Use the best quality eating or cooking chocolate you can afford.*

Toast the hazelnuts in the oven, then rub with a tea towel to remove the skins.

Stir the chopped hazelnuts into the icing, then pour over the base.

Triple-decker fudge slice

PREPARATION TIME: 25 MINUTES + REFRIGERATION I TOTAL COOKING TIME: 1 HOUR 10 MINUTES I MAKES 20 PIECES

100 g (3½ oz/¾ cup) plain (all-purpose) flour
3 tablespoons unsweetened cocoa powder
3 tablespoons caster (superfine) sugar
90 g (3¼ oz) unsalted butter, melted
1 tablespoon milk
½ teaspoon vanilla essence

VANILLA TOPPING
250 g (9 oz) cream cheese, cubed
90 g (3¼ oz/⅓ cup) caster (superfine) sugar
1 egg
1 teaspoon vanilla essence

CHOCOLATE TOPPING
125 g (4½ oz) milk chocolate, chopped
125 g (4½ oz) unsalted butter, chopped
2 eggs, lightly beaten
125 g (4½ oz/½ cup) caster (superfine) sugar
30 g (1 oz/¼ cup) plain (all-purpose) flour
icing (confectioners') sugar, to dust

1 Lightly grease a 28 x 18 cm (11¼ x 7 inch) shallow baking tin and line with baking paper, making sure the paper overhangs on two opposite sides.

2 Sift the flour, cocoa and sugar into a bowl. Add the butter, milk and vanilla and mix well to form a dough. Gently knead for 1 minute, adding more flour if sticky. Press into the prepared tin and refrigerate for 20 minutes.

3 Preheat the oven to 180°C (350°F/Gas 4). Bake the cocoa dough for 5–10 minutes, then leave to cool.

4 To make the vanilla topping, beat the cream cheese in a mixing bowl until smooth. Gradually beat in the sugar, then the egg and vanilla. Beat well, pour over the base and refrigerate.

5 To make the chocolate topping, melt the chocolate and butter in a small saucepan, stirring over very low heat until smooth. Mix together the eggs and sugar. Stir in the chocolate mixture and flour until just combined.

6 Pour the chocolate topping over the cold vanilla topping and smooth with a spoon. Reduce the oven to 160°C (315°F/Gas 2–3) and bake for 35–40 minutes, or until just set. Leave to cool completely, then refrigerate for 2 hours, or until firm. Dust with icing sugar before cutting and serving.

Use your fingers to press the mixture into the lined tin, making sure it is evenly spread.

Gradually add the sugar to the cream cheese, beating well.

Smooth the chocolate topping over the vanilla topping with the back of a spoon.

Mixed nut slice

PREPARATION TIME: 25 MINUTES + 30 MINUTES REFRIGERATION | TOTAL COOKING TIME: 50 MINUTES | MAKES 20 PIECES

215 g (7½ oz) plain (all-purpose) flour
2 tablespoons icing (confectioners') sugar
125 g (4½ oz) unsalted butter, chopped
1–2 tablespoons lemon juice or water
80 g (2¾ oz/½ cup) macadamia nuts
80 g (2¾ oz/½ cup) whole unblanched almonds
75 g (2½ oz/½ cup) pistachio nuts
70 g (2½ oz/½ cup) hazelnuts
2 eggs, lightly beaten
50 g (1¾ oz) unsalted butter, melted
60 g (2¼ oz/⅓ cup) lightly packed soft brown sugar
80 ml (2½ fl oz/⅓ cup) dark corn syrup
1 teaspoon vanilla essence
2 tablespoons cream

1 Lightly grease a 28 x 18 cm (11¼ x 7 inch) shallow baking tin and line with baking paper, making sure the paper overhangs on two opposite sides.

2 Process the flour, icing sugar and butter in a food processor until crumbs form. Add the lemon juice or water and process until the mixture just comes together. Wrap in plastic wrap and refrigerate for 30 minutes. Preheat the oven to 180°C (350°F/Gas 4). Roll the pastry out between two sheets of baking paper and fit to the base and sides of the tin. Trim away the excess pastry.

3 Cover the pastry with baking paper and fill with baking beads or uncooked rice. Bake for 10 minutes. Remove the paper and beads and bake the pastry base for 5–10 minutes longer, or until lightly golden. Cool completely.

4 Mix together the nuts and scatter over the pastry base.

5 Whisk together the remaining ingredients, pour over the nuts, then bake the slice for 25–30 minutes, or until set. Cool completely in the tin before lifting out to cut and serve.

Roll out the pastry between two sheets of baking paper until it is large enough to fit the tin.

Mix together the nuts and scatter them over the pastry base.

Banana hazelnut slice

PREPARATION TIME: 40 MINUTES + 30 MINUTES REFRIGERATION | TOTAL COOKING TIME: 45 MINUTES | MAKES 12 PIECES

125 g (4½ oz/1 cup) plain (all-purpose) flour
1½ teaspoons mixed (pumpkin pie) spice
2¼ tablespoons soft brown sugar
60 g (2¼ oz) unsalted butter
2 egg yolks
icing (confectioners') sugar, to dust

BANANA FILLING
60 g (2¼ oz) unsalted butter
60 g (2¼ oz/¼ cup) firmly packed soft brown
    sugar
2 bananas
1 egg
60 g (2¼ oz/½ cup) ground hazelnuts
30 g (1 oz/¼ cup) plain (all-purpose) flour
35 g (1¼ oz/¼ cup) hazelnuts, halved

1 Lightly grease a 35 x 11 cm (14 x 4¼ inch) loose-bottomed flan (tart) tin.

2 Place the flour, mixed spice and brown sugar in a food processor, add the butter, and process in short bursts until crumbly. Add the egg yolks and process until the dough just comes together. Wrap in plastic wrap and refrigerate for 30 minutes. Preheat the oven to 200°C (400°F/Gas 6).

3 Roll the pastry out between two sheets of baking paper to fit the tin and trim away the excess. Line with baking paper, fill with baking beads or uncooked rice, then bake for 8 minutes. Remove the beads and paper and bake the pastry for 5 minutes, or until lightly browned. Cool. Reduce the oven to 180°C (350°F/Gas 4).

4 To make the banana filling, beat the butter and sugar. Mash one of the bananas and stir into the beaten mixture with the egg. Stir in the ground hazelnuts and flour. Thinly slice the other banana and arrange over the pastry. Top with the banana filling and decorate with the hazelnut halves.

5 Bake for 30 minutes, or until golden brown and firm. Cool in the tin for 5 minutes, then on a wire rack. Dust lightly with icing sugar to serve.

Ease the pastry into the tin and trim the excess with a rolling pin or knife.

Thinly slice the other banana and arrange over the pastry base.

Pear and macadamia fingers

PREPARATION TIME: 25 MINUTES + 30 MINUTES REFRIGERATION | TOTAL COOKING TIME: 55 MINUTES | MAKES 20 PIECES

90 g (3¼ oz/¾ cup) plain (all-purpose) flour
25 g (1 oz) unsalted butter, chopped
1½ tablespoons ground almonds
1½ tablespoons icing (confectioners') sugar
1 egg yolk
¼ teaspoon vanilla essence

MACADAMIA TOPPING
100 g (3½ oz/¾ cup) macadamia nuts,
    roughly chopped
185 g (6½ oz/1 cup) lightly packed soft
    brown sugar
150 g (5½ oz) unsalted butter, chopped
1 teaspoon vanilla essence
100 g (3½ oz) dried pears, chopped
50 g (1¾ oz) chocolate chips

1   Place the flour, butter, ground almonds and icing sugar in a food processor and process until the mixture is crumbly. Add the egg yolk, vanilla and 1–2 teaspoons cold water to make the dough just come together. Turn out, gather into a ball and cover with plastic wrap. Refrigerate for 30 minutes.

2   Preheat the oven to 180°C (350°F/Gas 4). Lightly grease a 20 cm (8 inch) square cake tin and line the base and sides with baking paper. Roll out the dough to fit the base of the tin. Bake for 15 minutes, or until lightly browned. Leave to cool.

3   To make the macadamia topping, spread the macadamias on a baking tray and roast for 7 minutes, or until golden brown.

4   Put the brown sugar and butter in a saucepan and stir over low heat until the butter is melted and the sugar is dissolved. Bring to the boil, reduce the heat to low and cook for 1 minute, stirring. Remove from the heat and add the vanilla, pears, chocolate chips and macadamia nuts.

5   Spread the mixture over the pastry and bake for 30 minutes, or until bubbling all over. Leave the slice to cool completely in the tin before cutting into fingers to serve.

Roll out the pastry to fit the prepared tin and bake for 15 minutes, or until lightly browned.

Remove the saucepan from the heat and add the vanilla, pears, chocolate chips and nuts.

Spread the mixture over the pastry base and bake for 30 minutes.

Fruit and oat slice

PREPARATION TIME: 20 MINUTES + 10 MINUTES STANDING | TOTAL COOKING TIME: 1 HOUR | MAKES 24 PIECES

125 g (4½ oz) unsalted butter
95 g (3¼ oz/½ cup) lightly packed soft brown sugar
2 eggs, separated
160 g (5½ oz/1 cup) wholemeal (whole-wheat) self-raising flour
25 g (1 oz/¼ cup) wheatgerm
35 g (1¼ oz) dried apricots, finely chopped
60 ml (2 fl oz/¼ cup) boiling water

TOPPING
425 g (15 oz) tinned pie apples (see NOTE)
1 small zucchini (courgette), grated
45 g (1½ oz) rolled (porridge) oats
45 g (1½ oz/½ cup) desiccated coconut
2 tablespoons honey

1 Preheat the oven to 180°C (350°F/Gas 4). Lightly grease a 30 x 20 cm (12 x 8 inch) shallow baking tin. Line the base and sides with baking paper. Using electric beaters, beat the butter and sugar in a large bowl until light and creamy. Add the egg yolks and beat until combined. Sift the flour into the mixture, return the husks to the bowl, and mix with a flat-bladed knife. Add the wheatgerm and mix until a soft dough forms. Press mixture over the base of the prepared tin and smooth the surface. Bake for 12–15 minutes, or until golden.

2 Soak the apricots in a saucepan of boiling water for 10 minutes, or until almost all the liquid is absorbed.

3 Spread the apple over the base. Combine the undrained apricots with the zucchini, oats, coconut and honey in a mixing bowl. Using electric beaters, beat the egg whites in a clean, dry mixing bowl until stiff peaks form and gently fold into the mixture.

4 Spoon the mixture over the apples. Bake for 40–45 minutes, or until golden. Leave to cool in the tin, then cut into slices to serve.

NOTE: *Freshly cooked apples may be used instead of tinned apples.*

Make sure the flour and wheatgerm are well incorporated into the mixture.

Using a metal spoon, fold the beaten egg white into the topping mixture.

Cherry slice

PREPARATION TIME: 15 MINUTES | TOTAL COOKING TIME: 35 MINUTES | MAKES ABOUT 15 PIECES

250 g (9 oz/2 cups) plain (all-purpose) flour
60 g (2¼ oz/½ cup) icing (confectioners') sugar
250 g (9 oz) unsalted butter, chopped

TOPPING
30 g (1 oz) unsalted butter
90 g (3¼ oz/⅓ cup) caster (superfine) sugar
1 tablespoon milk
2 teaspoons vanilla essence
90 g (3¼ oz/¾ cup) chopped hazelnuts
150 g (5½ oz) sliced red glacé (candied)
    cherries

1   Preheat the oven to 210°C (415°F/Gas 6–7).
Lightly grease a 28 x 18 cm (11¼ x 7 inch)
shallow baking tin. Line the base with baking
paper, making sure the paper overhangs on two
opposite sides. Sift the flour and icing sugar into
a mixing bowl. Add the butter and, using your
fingertips, rub in until a dough forms. Press into
the prepared tin. Bake for 15 minutes, or until
light golden brown.

2   To make the topping, melt the butter in a
small saucepan and add the sugar, milk and
vanilla. Stir, without boiling, until the sugar
dissolves then bring to the boil. Remove from the
heat. Add the hazelnuts and cherries and stir.

3   Spread the topping over the base. Bake for
15–20 minutes, or until golden. Cut the slice into
squares while still warm and cool before serving.

STORAGE: *Store for up to 5 days in an airtight
container in a cool, dark place.*

Press the mixture firmly into the prepared tin with
your hands, making sure it is evenly distributed.

Add the sugar, milk and vanilla to the melted butter,
constantly stirring with a wooden spoon.

Remove the slice from the baking tin and cut into
squares while it is still warm.

Strawberry meringue slice

PREPARATION TIME: 30 MINUTES + REFRIGERATION | TOTAL COOKING TIME: 40 MINUTES | MAKES 12 PIECES

375 g (13 oz) fresh strawberries, hulled and
  sliced
1½ tablespoons grappa (see VARIATION)
2 tablespoons caster (superfine) sugar

BASE
125 g (4½ oz) unsalted butter, softened
90 g (3¼ oz/⅓ cup) caster (superfine) sugar
1 egg
½ teaspoon vanilla essence
90 g (3¼ oz/¾ cup) plain (all-purpose) flour
40 g (1½ oz/⅓ cup) self-raising flour

MERINGUE
2 egg whites
125 g (4½ oz/½ cup) caster (superfine) sugar
30 g (1 oz/⅓ cup) flaked almonds

1 Preheat the oven to 180°C (350°F/Gas 4).
Lightly grease a 28 x 18 cm (11¼ x 7 inch)
shallow baking tin and line with baking paper,
making sure the paper overhangs on two
opposite sides.

2 Mix the strawberries, grappa and sugar in
a mixing bowl, cover and refrigerate while
making the base.

3 To make the base, beat the butter and sugar
in a small mixing bowl with electric beaters until
light and fluffy. Add the egg and vanilla and mix
well. Sift the flours together and gently fold in.
Spread the mixture into the tin and bake for
15–20 minutes, or until pale golden. Leave to
cool slightly in the tin.

4 Drain the strawberries and spread them
over the warm base.

5 To make the meringue, beat the egg whites
with electric beaters in a small mixing bowl
until stiff peaks form. Gradually add the
sugar, a little at a time, beating well after each
addition. Spread the meringue mixture over the
strawberries and sprinkle with flaked almonds.

6 Bake for 15–20 minutes, or until lightly
coloured. Slice and serve warm.

STORAGE: *This slice is best eaten on the day
of making.*

VARIATION: *Vodka can be used instead of
grappa, if preferred.*

Mix together the strawberries, grappa and sugar
and leave in the fridge.

Spread the base mixture evenly in the tin and bake
until pale golden.

Spread the meringue mixture evenly over the
strawberries and sprinkle with almonds.

Spicy fruit cake slice

PREPARATION TIME: 25 MINUTES + 20 MINUTES REFRIGERATION | TOTAL COOKING TIME: 30 MINUTES | MAKES 16 PIECES

60 g (2¼ oz/½ cup) plain (all-purpose) flour
1 tablespoon cornflour (cornstarch)
1 tablespoon self-raising flour
50 g (1¾ oz) unsalted butter
2 tablespoons caster (superfine) sugar
1 egg yolk

FRUITY TOPPING
125 g (4½ oz) unsalted butter
125 g (4½ oz/½ cup) caster (superfine) sugar
1 egg
440 g (15½ oz) crumbled dark fruit cake or
  pudding
2 tablespoons raspberry jam
60 g (2¼ oz/½ cup) self-raising flour
1 tablespoon unsweetened cocoa powder
1 teaspoon ground cinnamon
1 teaspoon mixed (pumpkin pie) spice
icing (confectioners') sugar, to dust

1   Preheat the oven to 180°C (350°F/Gas 4).
Lightly grease a 30 x 20 cm (12 x 8 inch) shallow
baking tin and line with baking paper, making
sure the paper overhangs on two opposite sides.

2   Put the flours, butter and sugar in a food
processor and process until the mixture
resembles fine breadcrumbs. Add the egg yolk
and 1–2 teaspoons water (add more water
if necessary, to make the dough just come
together). Gather into a smooth ball and cover
with plastic wrap. Refrigerate for 20 minutes,
then roll the dough out between two sheets of
baking paper to fit the base of the tin.

3   To make the fruity topping, beat the butter
and sugar with electric beaters until light
and fluffy. Add the egg and beat until well
incorporated. Stir in the crumbled cake, jam,
flour, cocoa and spices and mix well. Spread the
topping over the pastry base and bake for about
30 minutes, or until a skewer inserted into the
centre comes out clean. Cool in the tin for
5 minutes before turning out onto a wire rack to
cool completely. Dust lightly with icing sugar
and serve.

After chilling the dough, roll it out between two sheets of baking paper.

Stir the crumbed cake, jam, flour, cocoa and spices into the creamed mixture with a metal spoon.

Chocolate dessert slice

PREPARATION TIME: 30 MINUTES | TOTAL COOKING TIME: 20 MINUTES + 2 HOURS REFRIGERATION | MAKES 16 SQUARES

200 g (7 oz) dark chocolate cream biscuits
50 g (1¾ oz) unsalted butter, melted
250 ml (9 fl oz/1 cup) milk
3 egg yolks
90 g (3¼ oz/⅓ cup) caster (superfine) sugar
2 tablespoons cornflour (cornstarch)
30 g (1 oz/¼ cup) unsweetened cocoa powder
1 tablespoon Marsala
250 g (9 oz/1 cup) mascarpone cheese
2½ teaspoons gelatine
1 tablespoon boiling water
50 g (1¾ oz) white chocolate shavings

1   Preheat the oven to 180°C (350°F/Gas 4). Lightly grease a 20 cm (8 inch) shallow square baking tin. Line the base and sides with baking paper, making sure the paper overhangs on two opposite sides.

2   Place the biscuits in a food processor and process until finely crushed. Add the butter and process until combined. Press the mixture firmly into the base of the prepared tin. Bake for 10 minutes, and leave to cool completely.

3   Heat the milk in a small saucepan until almost boiling. Remove from the heat. Whisk the egg yolks, sugar, cornflour, cocoa and 2 tablespoons of the milk in a small mixing bowl until creamy. Add the remaining milk gradually, beating constantly. Strain the mixture into the saucepan. Stir over a low heat for 5–8 minutes until the mixture thickens slightly and coats the back of a wooden spoon. Remove from the heat and stir in the Marsala. Pour into a mixing bowl and cover with plastic wrap. Cool to lukewarm and fold in the mascarpone until combined.

4   In a small bowl, dissolve the gelatine with 1 tablespoon of cold water and stand the bowl in hot water to soften the gelatine. Add to the custard. Stir until combined. Pour the custard onto the biscuit base, cover with plastic wrap and refrigerate for 2 hours. When set, carefully lift the slice from the tin. Cut into squares and decorate with the chocolate shavings.

Strain the mixture into the pan and stir until it is thick enough to coat the back of a wooden spoon.

Using a vegetable peeler, shave off chocolate from a block and use to decorate the slices.

Passionfruit marshmallow slice

PREPARATION TIME: 25 MINUTES + OVERNIGHT REFRIGERATION | TOTAL COOKING TIME: 30 MINUTES | MAKES 16 PIECES

150 g (5½ oz) unsalted butter
60 g (2¼ oz/¼ cup) caster (superfine) sugar
½ teaspoon vanilla essence
125 g (4½ oz/1 cup) plain (all-purpose) flour
60 g (2¼ oz/½ cup) self-raising flour

MARSHMALLOW TOPPING
125 ml (4 fl oz/½ cup) passionfruit pulp
250 g (9 oz) white marshmallows
125 ml (4 fl oz/½ cup) milk
2 tablespoons caster (superfine) sugar
2 teaspoons lemon juice
315 ml (10¾ fl oz/1¼ cups) whipping cream,
    lightly whipped

1   Preheat the oven to 180°C (350°F/Gas 4). Lightly grease a 28 x 18 cm (11¼ x 7 inch) shallow baking tin and line with baking paper, making sure the paper overhangs on two opposite sides.

2   Using electric beaters, beat the butter and sugar in a mixing bowl until light and creamy, and the sugar has dissolved. Stir in the vanilla. Sift the flours into a bowl, then fold into the butter mixture and mix to a soft dough. Knead gently to bring together.

3   Press the dough into the prepared tin and smooth with the back of a spoon. Lightly prick the dough and bake for 25 minutes, or until golden. Remove from the oven and leave to cool completely.

4   To make the topping, put the passionfruit, marshmallows, milk and sugar in a saucepan and stir over low heat until the marshmallows have melted.

5   Stir in the lemon juice and transfer to a bowl to cool. Refrigerate, stirring occasionally, for 30 minutes, or until slightly thickened. Quickly fold in the cream so the marshmallow doesn't set, then pour over the slice and refrigerate overnight, or until set. Cut into squares to serve.

STORAGE: *Store for up to 2 days in an airtight container in a cool, dark place.*

Press the dough into the tin, smooth the surface and prick with a fork.

Fold the whipped cream into the mixture quickly, so the marshmallow doesn't set.

Apple crumble slice

PREPARATION TIME: 20 MINUTES I TOTAL COOKING TIME: 40 MINUTES I MAKES 15 SQUARES

90 g (3¼ oz/¾ cup) self-raising flour
90 g (3¼ oz/¾ cup) plain (all-purpose) flour
90 g (3¼ oz/1 cup) desiccated coconut
250 g (9 oz) unsalted butter
140 g (5 oz/¾ cup) lightly packed soft brown
    sugar
410 g (14½ oz) tinned pie apples
35 g (1¼ oz/⅓ cup) rolled (porridge) oats
35 g (1¼ oz/¼ cup) currants
¼ teaspoon ground cinnamon

1 Preheat the oven to 180°C (350°F/Gas 4).
Lightly grease a 27 x 18 cm (10¾ x 7 inch) shallow
rectangular baking tin and line with baking paper,
making sure the paper overhangs on two opposite
sides. Sift the flours into a large mixing bowl and
add the coconut. Combine 200 g (7 oz) of the
butter and the sugar in a small saucepan. Stir over
low heat until the butter is melted and the sugar
is dissolved. Remove from the heat and pour the
mixture into the dry ingredients. Using a wooden
spoon, stir until well combined.

2 Reserve 1 cup of the mixture. Press the
remaining mixture into the prepared tin. Bake
for 10 minutes and leave to cool completely.

3 Spread the pie apple over the base. Combine
the reserved mixture, remaining butter, oats and
currants. Using fingertips, crumble the mixture
over the apple. Dust with the cinnamon. Bake
for 20 minutes, or until the crumble is golden
brown. Cool, lift from tin and cut into squares.

STORAGE: *The slice can be stored for up to*
2 days in an airtight container.

Using a wooden spoon, stir the melted butter and sugar into the sifted flours.

Place the mixture into the prepared tin, pressing firmly with the back of a spoon.

After the base has cooled, spread the pie apple over the top and sprinkle the crumble mixture over.

Chocolate carrot slice

PREPARATION TIME: 15 MINUTES I TOTAL COOKING TIME: 30 MINUTES I MAKES 32 TRIANGLES

125 g (4½ oz/1 cup) self-raising flour
1 teaspoon ground cinnamon
185 g (6½ oz/¾ cup) caster (superfine) sugar
55 g (2 oz/⅓ cup) finely grated carrot
190 g (6¾ oz) mixed dried fruit
95 g (3¼ oz) chocolate chips
30 g (1 oz/⅓ cup) desiccated coconut
2 eggs, lightly beaten
90 g (3¼ oz) unsalted butter, melted
40 g (1½ oz/⅓ cup) chopped walnuts

CREAM CHEESE ICING
125 g (4½ oz) cream cheese
30 g (1 oz) unsalted butter
185 g (6½ oz/1½ cups) icing (confectioners')
    sugar, sifted
1 teaspoon hot water

1   Preheat the oven to 180°C (350°F/Gas 4).
Lightly grease a 23 cm (9 inch) square shallow
baking tin and line with baking paper, making
sure the paper overhangs two opposite sides. Sift
the flour and cinnamon into a large mixing bowl.
Add the sugar, carrot, mixed fruit, chocolate
chips and coconut and stir until just combined.
Add the egg and butter. Stir until the mixture is
just combined.

2   Spread the mixture into the prepared tin and
smooth the surface. Bake for 30 minutes, or until
golden. Cool in the tin and then turn out.

3   To make the cream cheese icing (frosting),
beat the cream cheese and butter with electric
beaters in a small bowl until smooth. Add the
icing sugar and beat for 2 minutes or until the
mixture is light and fluffy. Add the water and
beat until combined. Using a flat-bladed knife,
spread the icing on top of the slice and sprinkle
with walnuts. Cut into 16 squares, then cut each
square into triangles.

STORAGE: *The slice may be stored for up to
2 days in an airtight container or up to 2 months
in the freezer, without icing.*

VARIATION: *Sprinkle the icing (frosting) with
grated chocolate if desired.*

Use a rubber spatula to spread the mixture evenly
around the prepared tin.

After the slice has cooled, use a flat-bladed knife to
spread the icing over the top.

Coconut pineapple squares

PREPARATION TIME: 20 MINUTES | TOTAL COOKING TIME: 20 MINUTES | MAKES 12 SQUARES

250 g (9 oz) oatmeal biscuits, crushed
90 g (3¼ oz/1½ cups) shredded coconut
250 g (9 oz) chopped glacé (candied)
    pineapple
90 g (3¼ oz/1 cup) flaked almonds
200 ml (7 fl oz) sweetened condensed milk
100 g (3½ oz) unsalted butter, melted

COCONUT ICING
60 g (2¼ oz) unsalted butter, softened
few drops coconut essence
90 g (3¼ oz/¾ cup) icing (confectioners')
    sugar, sifted
1 tablespoon milk
90 g (3¼ oz) toasted flaked coconut (see
    HINT)

1   Preheat the oven to 180°C (350°F/Gas 4).
Lightly grease a shallow 27 x 18 cm (10¾ x
7 inch) rectangular baking tin and line with
baking paper. Combine the crushed biscuits,
coconut, pineapple and almonds in a large
mixing bowl. Make a well in the centre of the
ingredients and pour in the condensed milk and
butter. Stir until well combined.

2   Press the mixture firmly into the prepared
tin. Bake for 20 minutes, or until the top is
lightly golden. Leave to cool in the tin.

3   To make the coconut icing (frosting), beat
the butter and coconut essence with electric
beaters in a mixing bowl until light and creamy.
Add the icing sugar and milk. Beat until smooth
and fluffy. Spread the icing evenly over the slice
and sprinkle with the toasted coconut. Cut
into squares to serve.

STORAGE: *The slice may be stored for up to
3 days in an airtight container or up to 2 months
in the freezer, without icing.*

HINT: *Toast the coconut by simply spreading
it on a baking tray and baking for 5 minutes,
or until golden.*

Place all the ingredients for the base in a large
mixing bowl and stir until well combined.

Bake the base for 20 minutes, or until the top is
lightly golden, then set aside to cool.

Using electric beaters, beat the icing ingredients
until smooth and fluffy.

White chocolate and mango slice

PREPARATION TIME: 25 MINUTES I TOTAL COOKING TIME: 45 MINUTES I MAKES 10 PIECES

100 g (3½ oz) unsalted butter
125 g (4½ oz/½ cup) caster (superfine) sugar
2 eggs, lightly beaten
1 teaspoon vanilla essence
185 g (6½ oz/1½ cups) self-raising flour
125 ml (4 fl oz/½ cup) buttermilk
100 g (3½ oz) white chocolate, grated
2 x 425 g (15 oz) tinned mango slices, drained,
   or 2 large fresh mangoes, sliced
60 g (2¼ oz/¼ cup) caster (superfine) sugar,
   extra

1   Preheat the oven to 180°C (350°F/Gas 4). Lightly grease a 28 x 18 cm (11¼ x 7 inch) shallow baking tin and line with baking paper, making sure the paper overhangs on two opposite sides.

2   Using electric beaters, beat the butter and sugar in a mixing bowl until light and creamy. Gradually add the egg and vanilla, beating until well combined.

3   Using a metal spoon, alternately fold the sifted flour and buttermilk into the mixture, stirring until just combined. Add the grated chocolate. Pour into the prepared tin and smooth the surface. Arrange the mango over the top. Place the tin on an oven tray to catch any drips. Bake for 35–40 minutes, or until golden brown.

4   Put the extra sugar in a small saucepan with 1 tablespoon water and stir over low heat until dissolved. Bring to the boil, then simmer for 1–2 minutes. Brush the syrup over the slice as soon as it comes out of the oven. Cut into pieces and serve hot.

Fold the flour and buttermilk into the mixture, then add the chocolate.

Brush the syrup over the slice as soon as it comes out of the oven.

Raspberry linzer slice

PREPARATION TIME: 30 MINUTES | TOTAL COOKING TIME: 45 MINUTES | MAKES 20 PIECES

90 g (3¼ oz) unsalted butter
125 g (4½ oz/½ cup) caster (superfine) sugar
1 teaspoon vanilla essence
1 egg, lightly beaten
85 g (3 oz/⅔ cup) plain (all-purpose) flour
40 g (1½ oz/⅓ cup) self-raising flour
240 g (8½ oz/¾ cup) raspberry jam, warmed
Icing (confectioners') sugar, to dust

HAZELNUT TOPPING
125 g (4½ oz) unsalted butter
90 g (3¼ oz/⅓ cup) caster (superfine) sugar
1 egg, lightly beaten
60 g (2¼ oz/½ cup) plain (all-purpose) flour
1 tablespoon custard powder
1 tcaspoon baking powder
120 g (4¼ oz) firmly packed plain cake crumbs
60 g (2¼ oz) ground hazelnuts
80 ml (2½ fl oz/⅓ cup) milk

1 Preheat the oven to 180°C (350°F/Gas 4). Lightly grease a 30 x 20 cm (12 x 8 inch) shallow baking tin and line with baking paper, making sure the paper overhangs on two opposite sides.

2 Using electric beaters, beat the butter, sugar and vanilla in a mixing bowl until light and creamy. Add the egg to the mixture, a little at a time, beating well after each addition.

3 Sift the flours and fold into the mixture with a metal spoon. Spread into the prepared tin and spread evenly with the raspberry jam.

4 To make the hazelnut topping, beat the butter and sugar with electric beaters until light and creamy. Add the egg gradually, beating well. Sift the flour, custard powder and baking powder and fold into the mixture with the cake crumbs and ground hazelnuts. Fold in the milk and spread the mixture over the jam. Bake for 45 minutes, or until firm and golden brown. Leave to cool in the tin before cutting to serve.

Spread the mixture evenly into the prepared tin, then spread with jam.

Spread the hazelnut topping over the jam and bake for 45 minutes.

Choc-peppermint slice

PREPARATION TIME: 25 MINUTES + 30 MINUTES REFRIGERATION | TOTAL COOKING TIME: 20 MINUTES | MAKES 24 PIECES

100 g (3½ oz/¾ cup) self-raising flour
30 g (1 oz/¼ cup) unsweetened cocoa powder
45 g (1½ oz/½ cup) desiccated coconut
60 g (2¼ oz/¼ cup) sugar
140 g (5 oz) unsalted butter, melted
1 egg, lightly beaten

PEPPERMINT FILLING
185 g (6½ oz/1½ cups) icing (confectioners')
    sugar, sifted
30 g (1 oz) white vegetable shortening, melted
2 tablespoons milk
½ teaspoon peppermint essence

CHOCOLATE TOPPING
185 g (6½ oz) dark chocolate, chopped
30 g (1 oz) white vegetable shortening

1 Preheat the oven to 180°C (350°F/Gas 4). Lightly grease a 28 x 18 cm (11¼ x 7 inch) shallow baking tin. Line the tin with baking paper, making sure the paper overhangs the two longer sides. This makes it easy to lift the cooked slice out of the tin.

2 Sift the flour and cocoa into a bowl. Stir in the coconut and sugar, then add the butter and egg and mix well. Press the mixture firmly into the tin. Bake for 15 minutes, then press down with the back of a spoon and leave to cool.

3 For the peppermint filling, sift the icing sugar into a bowl. Stir in the shortening, milk and peppermint essence. Spread over the base and refrigerate for 5–10 minutes, or until firm.

4 For the chocolate topping, put the chocolate and shortening in a heatproof bowl. Half-fill a saucepan with water, bring to the boil, then remove from the heat. Sit the bowl over the saucepan, making sure the base of the bowl does not touch the water. Stir occasionally until the chocolate and shortening have melted and combined, then leave for 4–5 minutes until slightly thickened. Spread evenly over the filling. Refrigerate the slice for 20 minutes, or until the chocolate topping is firm. Carefully lift the slice from the tin, using the paper as handles. Cut into pieces with a warm knife to give clean edges.

STORAGE: *Store in an airtight container in the refrigerator.*

Sift the dry ingredients into a bowl, then add the melted butter and egg.

Using a flat-bladed knife spread the peppermint filling evenly over the cooled base.

Stir the chocolate and shortening in a heatproof bowl over simmering water.

Date and peach slice

PREPARATION TIME: 15 MINUTES + 30 MINUTES SOAKING | TOTAL COOKING TIME: 40 MINUTES | MAKES 16 PIECES

200 g (7 oz) dried peaches
125 g (4½ oz/1 cup) self-raising flour
125 g (4½ oz/1 cup) plain (all-purpose) flour
90 g (3¼ oz/½ cup) lightly packed soft brown
    sugar
110 g (3½ oz/½ cup) raw (demerara) sugar
1½ teaspoons ground cinnamon
45 g (1½ oz/¾ cup) shredded coconut
125 g (4½ oz) dates, chopped
125 g (4½ oz) unsalted butter, melted

1 Lightly grease a 23 cm (9 inch) shallow square baking tin and line with baking paper, making sure the paper overhangs on two opposite sides.

2 Roughly chop the peaches and place in a bowl. Cover the peaches with boiling water and leave to soak for 30 minutes. Preheat the oven to 180°C (350°F/Gas 4). Drain the peaches, reserving 125 ml (4 fl oz/½ cup) of the liquid.

3 Place the flours, sugars, cinnamon, coconut and dates in a large mixing bowl. Add the melted butter, peaches and reserved liquid and stir gently until only just combined.

4 Spread the mixture into the prepared tin and bake for 35–40 minutes, or until golden brown and a skewer inserted into the centre of the slice comes out clean. Cool in the tin for 5 minutes before turning out onto a wire rack to cool completely.

Use kitchen scissors or a sharp knife to roughly chop the dried peaches.

Put the flours, sugars, cinnamon, coconut and dates in a large mixing bowl.

Add the butter, peaches and reserved liquid and stir until just combined. Do not overmix.

Ginger delight slice

PREPARATION TIME: 20 MINUTES + COOLING | TOTAL COOKING TIME: 50 MINUTES | MAKES 16 PIECES

100 g (3½ oz) glacé (candied) ginger
220 g (7¾ oz/1¼ cups) plain (all-purpose) flour
220 g (7¾ oz/1 cup) raw (demerara) sugar
160 g (5½ oz) unsalted butter, melted
1 egg

GINGER ICING
80 g (2¾ oz) unsalted butter
1 tablespoon golden syrup (if unavailable,
    substitute with half honey and half dark
    corn syrup)
90 g (3¼ oz/¾ cup) icing (confectioners') sugar
1 teaspoon ground ginger
40 g (1½ oz/¼ cup) chopped macadamia nuts,
    toasted

1 Preheat the oven to 180°C (350°F/Gas 4). Lightly grease a 19 cm (7½ inch) square baking tin and line with baking paper, making sure the paper overhangs on two opposite sides.

2 Toss the glacé ginger in 1–2 tablespoons of the flour, then chop finely. Put the ginger in a mixing bowl with the remaining flour, sugar, melted butter, egg, and a pinch of salt and mix well.

3 Press the mixture evenly into the prepared tin and smooth the surface. Bake for 35–40 minutes, or until firm and golden brown. Cool in the tin for 20 minutes before lifting out.

4 To make the ginger icing (frosting), mix the butter, golden syrup, icing sugar and ginger over low heat. Stirring often, bring just to the boil then remove from the heat. Spread over the base and sprinkle with macadamias. Cool before cutting.

Toss the ginger in a little flour to stop it sticking to the knife when chopped.

Mix the ginger, flour, sugar, melted butter, egg and salt in a bowl.

Stir the ginger icing until it comes to the boil, then remove from the heat.

Rocky road slice

PREPARATION TIME: 35 MINUTES + COOLING | TOTAL COOKING TIME: 25–30 MINUTES | MAKES 16 PIECES

165 g (5¾ oz) unsalted butter

40 g (1½ oz/⅓ cup) icing (confectioners') sugar, sifted

125 g (4½ oz/1 cup) self-raising flour

2 tablespoons unsweetened cocoa powder

250 g (9 oz) coloured marshmallows

100 g (3½ oz) glacé (candied) cherries, halved (see VARIATION)

200 g (7 oz) dark chocolate, chopped

15 g (½ oz) white vegetable shortening

1 Preheat the oven to 160°C (315°F/Gas 2–3). Lightly grease two 26 x 8 x 4.5 cm (10½ x 3¼ x 1¾ inch) loaf (bar) tins and line with baking paper. Beat the butter and icing sugar in a large mixing bowl until light and creamy. Sift in the flour and cocoa and fold in with a metal spoon. Mix until well combined. Divide the mixture between both prepared tins. Press the mixture evenly into the tins using fingertips. Bake for 25–30 minutes, or until lightly coloured. Leave to cool in the tins.

2 Scatter the marshmallows and cherries on top of the bases.

3 Place the chocolate and shortening in a heatproof bowl. Stand over a saucepan of simmering water, making sure the base does not touch the water, and stir until the mixture is smooth. Cool slightly.

4 Spoon the mixture over both slices. Tap the tins gently on a bench to distribute the chocolate evenly. Allow the chocolate to set and cut into 2–3 cm (¾–1¼ inch) slices.

STORAGE: *The slice may be stored in an airtight container for up to 4 days.*

VARIATION: *Sprinkle 35 g (1¼ oz/¼ cup) roughly chopped mixed nuts over the cherries and marshmallows before spooning on the chocolate topping.*

HINT: *If you have refrigerated the slice to set the chocolate, allow it to come to room temperature before cutting.*

Leave the base in the tin to cool slightly then scatter the marshmallows and glacé cherries on top.

Melt the chocolate and shortening in a heatproof bowl set over a saucepan of simmering water.

Spoon the melted chocolate mixture evenly over the slices then leave to set.

Pineapple shortbread

PREPARATION TIME: 15 MINUTES + 15 MINUTES COOLING | TOTAL COOKING TIME: 30 MINUTES | MAKES 20 PIECES

150 g (5½ oz) unsalted butter, melted
125 g (4½ oz/½ cup) caster (superfine) sugar
2 eggs, lightly beaten
155 g (5½ oz/1¼ cups) plain (all-purpose) flour
½ teaspoon baking powder
2 tablespoons milk

PINEAPPLE CRISP
60 g (2¼ oz) unsalted butter, softened
95 g (3¼ oz/½ cup) lightly packed soft brown
    sugar
440 g (15½ oz) tinned crushed pineapples,
    very well drained (see NOTE)
60 g (2¼ oz/½ cup) chopped walnuts

1 Preheat the oven to 180°C (350°F/Gas 4). Line a lightly greased 28 x 18 cm (11¼ x 7 inch) shallow baking tin with baking paper, making sure the paper overhangs on two opposite sides.

2 Using electric beaters, beat the butter and sugar in a mixing bowl until light and creamy. Add the egg, a little at a time, beating thoroughly after each addition.

3 Sift the flour and baking powder with a pinch of salt and gently fold into the creamed mixture. Fold in the milk. Spread evenly into the tin and bake for 25 minutes, or until lightly golden. Cool for 15 minutes. Preheat the grill (broiler) to high.

4 To make the pineapple crisp, beat the butter and sugar until just combined, then stir in the pineapple and walnuts. Spread gently over the shortbread base, then place under the hot grill (broiler) for about 5 minutes, or until the topping bubbles and caramelises.

5 Leave to cool for a few minutes before cutting into pieces.

STORAGE: *Will keep for up to 3 days in an airtight container.*

NOTE: *Make sure the pineapple is drained thoroughly or it will make the base soggy.*

Fold the sifted flour, baking powder and salt, and the milk into the mixture until well combined.

Spread the pineapple crisp over the shortbread base and grill for 5 minutes.

Sour cream and cherry slice

PREPARATION TIME: 30 MINUTES + 1 HOUR REFRIGERATION | TOTAL COOKING TIME: 30 MINUTES | MAKES 15 PIECES

200 g (7 oz) sweet biscuits, crushed
1 teaspoon ground cinnamon
90 g (3¼ oz) unsalted butter, melted
2 x 425 g (15 oz) tinned pitted dark cherries
2 x 300 g (10½ oz) cartons sour cream
90 g (3¼ oz/⅓ cup) caster (superfine) sugar
2 eggs, lightly beaten

1 Lightly grease a 30 x 20 cm (12 x 8 inch) shallow baking tin and line with baking paper, making sure the paper overhangs on two opposite sides. Preheat the oven to 160°C (315°F/Gas 2–3).

2 Place the biscuit crumbs, cinnamon and butter in a mixing bowl and mix until well combined. Press the mixture firmly into the prepared tin. Refrigerate for 30 minutes, or until firm.

3 Drain the cherries, rinse well and pat dry with paper towels. Cut the cherries in half and scatter over the biscuit base. Mix together the sour cream, sugar and egg and pour over the cherries.

4 Bake for about 30 minutes, or until the topping has just set. Allow to cool, then refrigerate for 30 minutes, or until firm, before lifting out to cut.

Use the back of a spoon to press the biscuit base firmly into the tin.

Cut the cherries in half and scatter evenly over the biscuit base.

Lemon ginger slice

PREPARATION TIME: 40 MINUTES + 2–3 HOURS REFRIGERATION | TOTAL COOKING TIME: 30 MINUTES | MAKES 15 PIECES

200 g (7 oz) gingernut biscuits
90 g (3¼ oz) unsalted butter, melted
1 lemon
125 g (4½ oz/½ cup) sugar
125 ml (4 fl oz/½ cup) water

LEMON FILLING
100 g (3½ oz) unsalted butter, chopped
6 egg yolks
125 g (4½ oz/½ cup) caster (superfine) sugar
80 ml (2½ fl oz/⅓ cup) lemon juice
2 teaspoons finely grated lemon zest
2 teaspoons gelatine
125 ml (4 fl oz/½ cup) whipped cream

1 Lightly grease a 28 x 18 cm (11¼ x 7 inch) shallow baking tin and line with baking paper, making sure the paper overhangs on two opposite sides. Finely crush the biscuits in a food processor, then add the melted butter and process in short bursts. Place into the prepared tin and smooth with the back of a spoon. Refrigerate until ready to use.

2 To make the lemon filling, stir the butter, egg yolks, sugar, lemon juice and zest in a heatproof bowl set over a saucepan of simmering water for 15 minutes, or until the mixture is smooth and thick. Take care not to overheat or the mixture may curdle. Set aside to cool slightly.

3 Place 1 tablespoon water in a small mixing bowl and sprinkle with the gelatine. Stand the bowl in hot water to soften the gelatine, then whisk with a fork to dissolve. Stir into the lemon mixture. Leave to cool at room temperature, stirring now and then—do not refrigerate. Gently fold in the whipped cream. Spread the mixture over the biscuit base and smooth the surface with the back of a spoon. Refrigerate for 2–3 hours, or until set.

4 Cut 8 thin slices from the lemon. Put the sugar in a small saucepan with the water and stir without boiling for 5 minutes, or until the sugar dissolves completely. Add the lemon slices, bring the sugar syrup to the boil then reduce the heat and simmer for another 10 minutes. Remove the lemon slices, drain and cool on a wire rack, then cut into halves or quarters. Cut the slice into squares and top each one with a lemon piece.

Use a light touch to fold the whipped cream into the lemon mixture.

Leave the lemon slices to drain on a wire rack until they are cooled.

Fudgy coconut fingers

PREPARATION TIME: 20 MINUTES + COOLING | TOTAL COOKING TIME: 25 MINUTES | MAKES 16 PIECES

150 g (5½ oz/1 cup) plain (all-purpose) flour
1 tablespoon unsweetened cocoa powder
125 g (4½ oz/½ cup) caster (superfine) sugar
90 g (3¼ oz/1 cup) desiccated coconut
185 g (6½ oz) unsalted butter, melted
1 teaspoon vanilla essence
125 g (4½ oz) dark chocolate, chopped
2 tablespoons sour cream
30 g (1 oz/½ cup) flaked coconut, lightly
   toasted

1   Preheat the oven to 180°C (350°F/Gas 4).
Lightly grease a 28 x 18 cm (11¼ x 7 inch)
shallow baking tin and line with baking paper,
making sure the paper overhangs on two
opposite sides.

2   Sift the flour and cocoa into a large mixing
bowl. Add the sugar and desiccated coconut
and mix until well combined. Add the butter and
vanilla and mix until well combined. Press firmly
into the prepared tin and bake for 20 minutes, or
until firm and golden brown. Leave to cool
in the tin.

3   Stir the chocolate and sour cream in a
heatproof bowl over a saucepan of simmering
water until melted. Spread over the base and
sprinkle with the coconut. Leave for 20 minutes
before cutting into fingers.

STORAGE: *Will keep in an airtight container for
up to 4 days.*

Sift the flour and cocoa powder together into a large mixing bowl.

Press the mixture firmly into the prepared tin, then bake for 20 minutes.

Stir the chocolate and sour cream in a heatproof bowl over simmering water.

Jaffa fudge slice

PREPARATION TIME: 20 MINUTES + 40 MINUTES REFRIGERATION | TOTAL COOKING TIME: 3 MINUTES | MAKES 18 PIECES

200 g (7 oz) plain sweet chocolate biscuits
125 g (4½ oz/1 cup) chopped walnuts
125 g (4½ oz) dark chocolate, chopped
60 g (2¼ oz/½ cup) icing (confectioners')
    sugar
125 g (4½ oz) unsalted butter
1 tablespoon grated orange zest
125 g (4½ oz) dark chocolate, extra, melted

1   Lightly grease a 28 x 18 cm (11¼ x 7 inch) shallow baking tin and line with baking paper or foil, making sure the paper or foil overhangs on two opposite sides.

2   Place the biscuits and walnuts in a food processor and process until the mixture resembles coarse breadcrumbs. Transfer to a large mixing bowl and make a well in the centre.

3   Put the chopped chocolate, sifted icing sugar and butter in a small saucepan and stir over low heat until melted and smooth. Remove from the heat, stir in the orange zest, then pour into the biscuit mixture and stir until well combined.

4   Press the mixture firmly into the prepared tin. Refrigerate for 10 minutes. Spread the melted chocolate over and chill for 30 minutes to set.

STORAGE: *This slice can be kept in an airtight container for up to a week.*

Pour the chocolate mixture into the processed biscuits and walnuts.

Press firmly into the tin and then refrigerate for 10 minutes before covering with melted chocolate.

Chocolate hazelnut wedges

PREPARATION TIME: 30 MINUTES I TOTAL COOKING TIME: 50 MINUTES I MAKES 16 WEDGES

150 g (5½ oz) unsalted butter

60 g (2¼ oz/½ cup) icing (confectioners') sugar

40 g (1½ oz) ground hazelnuts (see VARIATION)

155 g (5½ oz/1¼ cups) plain (all-purpose) flour

50 g (1¾ oz/⅓ cup) dark chocolate melts (buttons)

80 g (2¾ oz) white chocolate melts (buttons)

1   Preheat the oven to 150°C (300°F/Gas 2). Lightly grease a shallow 20 cm (8 inch) round, fluted flan (tart) tin. Using electric beaters, beat the butter and icing sugar in a large mixing bowl until light and creamy. Add the ground hazelnuts and beat until combined. Using a metal spoon, fold in the sifted flour. Mix well.

2   Press the mixture evenly into the prepared tin and smooth the surface. Score into 16 wedges, using a sharp knife. Bake for 30 minutes, or until pale golden. Stand in the tin to cool.

3   Carefully remove the shortbread from the round tin. Using a sharp knife, cut it into scored wedges.

4   Place the dark chocolate in a small heatproof bowl. Stand over a saucepan of simmering water and stir until the chocolate is melted and smooth. Leave to cool slightly. Spoon the chocolate into a small paper piping (icing) bag and seal the open end. Snip off the tip. Pipe a wide strip down the centre of each wedge. Melt the white chocolate melts in the same way as the dark chocolate. Pipe a white zigzag pattern over the dark chocolate strip. Leave to set.

STORAGE: *Store wedges in an airtight container in a cool, dry place for up to 3 days.*

VARIATION: *Use ground almonds or walnuts instead of hazelnuts.*

Score the shortbread into 16 wedges before baking to make it easier to cut later.

After the shortbread has cooled, remove from the tin and cut into wedges.

Place wedges on a wire rack and decorate with the melted chocolate.

Pear, pecan and cheese slice

PREPARATION TIME: 25 MINUTES | TOTAL COOKING TIME: 45 MINUTES | MAKES 9 PIECES

30 g (1 oz/¼ cup) sultanas (golden raisins)
1 tablespoon Marsala or brandy
200 g (7 oz/1⅔ cups) self-raising flour
90 g (3¼ oz/⅓ cup) caster (superfine) sugar
80 g (2¾ oz) unsalted butter
1 egg
2 tablespoons chopped pecans
825 g (1 lb 13 oz) tinned pears, well drained
    and cubed
1 teaspoon vanilla essence
¼ teaspoon ground cinnamon

CHEESE FILLING
250 g (9 oz) cottage cheese
2 tablespoons sugar
2 eggs
2 tablespoons grated lemon zest
½ teaspoon vanilla essence
2 tablespoons plain (all-purpose) flour

1   Preheat the oven to 180°C (350°F/Gas 4). Lightly grease a 23 cm (9 inch) square shallow baking tin and line with baking paper, making sure the paper overhangs on two opposite sides.

2   Soak the sultanas in the Marsala in a bowl.

3   Place the flour, sugar and butter in a food processor and process for 15 seconds, or until the mixture resembles fine breadcrumbs. Add the egg and process again. Transfer a third of the mixture to a bowl, stir in the pecans and set aside. Spread the remaining mixture into the tin, pressing firmly and evenly.

4   Put the pear in a bowl, add the vanilla and the cinnamon and mix well. Spread over the pastry base.

5   To make the cheese filling, blend the cottage cheese and sugar in a food processor until just smooth. Add the remaining ingredients and process until smooth. Stir in the sultanas and Marsala, then spoon over the pears.

6   Sprinkle the remaining base mixture over the top. Bake for 40–45 minutes, or until golden and set. Leave to cool before cutting.

Spread the pear mixture over the base and spoon over the cheese filling.

Sprinkle the remaining pecan mixture over the top and bake until golden and set.

Choc-nut triangles

PREPARATION TIME: 25 MINUTES I TOTAL COOKING TIME: 20 MINUTES I MAKES 16 PIECES

125 g (4½ oz/1 cup) self-raising flour
2 tablespoons unsweetened cocoa powder
125 g (4½ oz/½ cup) caster (superfine) sugar
60 g (2¼ oz/⅔ cup) desiccated coconut
125 g (4½ oz) unsalted butter, melted
1 teaspoon vanilla essence
125 g (4½ oz) chopped pecans or walnuts

CHOCOLATE ICING
125 g (4½ oz/1 cup) icing (confectioners')
   sugar
1 tablespoon unsweetened cocoa powder
15 g (½ oz) unsalted butter, melted
1½–2 tablespoons milk
60 g (2¼ oz/½ cup) chopped pecans or walnuts

1   Preheat the oven to 180°C (350°F/Gas 4).
Lightly grease a 28 x 18 cm (11¼ x 7 inch)
shallow baking tin and line with baking paper,
making sure the paper overhangs on two
opposite sides.

2   Sift the flour and cocoa into a large mixing
bowl. Stir in the sugar and coconut. Add the
melted butter, vanilla and nuts and stir until well
combined. Press the mixture firmly and evenly
into the prepared tin. Bake for 20 minutes,
or until golden brown. Allow the slice to cool
completely before removing from the tin.

3   To make the chocolate icing (frosting), sift
the icing sugar and cocoa into a mixing bowl.
Add the butter and enough milk to make
a smooth, spreadable icing. Mix until well
combined. Spread evenly over the cooled base,
using a flat-bladed knife. Sprinkle with the
nuts and leave to set for about 1 hour. Cut into
triangles using a sharp knife.

Using your fingertips, press the mixture firmly and evenly into the slice tin.

Spread the chocolate icing over the base with a flat-bladed knife.

Little cakes
and scones

Chocolate hazelnut friands

PREPARATION TIME: 20 MINUTES | TOTAL COOKING TIME: 40 MINUTES | MAKES 12

200 g (7 oz) whole hazelnuts
185 g (6½ oz) unsalted butter
6 egg whites
155 g (5½ oz/1¼ cups) plain (all-purpose)
    flour
30 g (1 oz/¼ cup) unsweetened cocoa powder
250 g (9 oz/2 cups) icing (confectioners')
    sugar
icing (confectioners') sugar, extra, to dust

1   Preheat the oven to 200°C (400°F/Gas 6). Lightly grease twelve 125 ml (4 fl oz/½ cup) friand or muffin tins. Spread the hazelnuts out on a baking tray. Bake for 8–10 minutes, or until fragrant, taking care not to burn the hazelnuts. Place in a clean tea towel (dish towel) and rub vigorously to loosen the skins. Cool, then process in a food processor until finely ground.

2   Place the butter in a small pan and melt over medium heat, then cook for 3–4 minutes, or until the butter turns a deep golden colour. Strain any dark solids and set aside to cool (the colour will become deeper on standing).

3   Lightly whisk the egg whites in a clean, dry bowl until frothy but not firm. Sift the flour, cocoa and icing sugar into a large mixing bowl and stir in the ground hazelnuts. Make a well in the centre and add the egg whites and butter and mix until combined.

4   Spoon the mixture into the prepared tins until three-quarters filled. Bake for 20–25 minutes, or until a skewer inserted into the centre comes out clean. Leave in the tin for a few minutes, then cool on a wire rack. Dust with icing sugar, to serve.

Cook the butter until it turns a deep golden colour, then strain and discard any dark solids.

Spoon the friand mixture into the greased tins until three-quarters filled.

Coffee cupcakes

PREPARATION TIME: 15 MINUTES I TOTAL COOKING TIME: 30 MINUTES I MAKES 24

195 g (6¾ oz) unsalted butter, softened
125 g (4½ oz/⅔ cup) lightly packed soft brown
   sugar
2 eggs
1 tablespoon coffee and chicory essence
155 g (5½ oz/1¼ cups) self-raising flour
100 ml (3½ fl oz) buttermilk
125 g (4½ oz/1 cup) icing (confectioners')
   sugar
1½ tablespoons boiling water
chocolate-coated coffee beans, to decorate
   (optional)

1   Preheat the oven to 150°C (300°F/Gas 2).
Line two 12-hole mini muffin tins with paper
cases. Beat 185 g (6½ oz) of the butter and the
brown sugar with electric beaters until light and
creamy. Add the eggs one at a time, beating well
after each addition. Mix in 3 teaspoons of the
coffee and chicory essence.

2   Fold the flour and a pinch of salt alternately
with the buttermilk into the creamed mixture
until combined. Spoon evenly into the paper
cases and bake for 25–30 minutes, or until just
springy to the touch. Leave to cool in the tins.

3   To make the icing, combine the remaining
butter, remaining essence, the icing sugar and
boiling water in a small mixing bowl. Spread a
little chocolate icing over each cupcake with a
flat-bladed knife.

Using electric beaters, cream the butter and sugar
before adding the eggs.

Spoon the mixture into the paper cases and bake
until just springy to the touch.

Individual sticky date cakes

PREPARATION TIME: 10 MINUTES | TOTAL COOKING TIME: 30 MINUTES | MAKES 8

270 g (9½ oz/1⅔ cups) stoned dates, chopped
1 teaspoon bicarbonate of soda (baking soda)
150 g (5½ oz) unsalted butter, chopped
185 g (6½ oz/1½ cups) self-raising flour
265 g (9¼ oz) firmly packed soft brown sugar
2 eggs, lightly beaten
2 tablespoons golden syrup (if unavailable,
    substitute with half honey and half dark
    corn syrup)
185 ml (6 fl oz/¾ cup) cream

1   Preheat the oven to 180°C (350°F/Gas 4).
Grease six 250 ml (9 fl oz/1 cup) muffin holes.
Place the dates and 250 ml (9 fl oz/1 cup) water
in a saucepan, bring to the boil, then remove
from the heat and stir in the bicarbonate of soda.
Add 60 g (2¼ oz) of the butter and stir until
completely dissolved.

2   Sift the flour into a large mixing bowl, add
125 g (4½ oz/⅔ cup) of the sugar and stir. Make
a well in the centre, add the date mixture and
egg and stir until just combined. Spoon the
mixture evenly into the prepared holes and bake
for 20 minutes, or until a skewer comes out clean
when inserted into the centre of the cake.

3   To make the sauce, place the golden syrup
and cream with the remaining butter and sugar
in a small saucepan and stir over low heat for
3–4 minutes, or until the sugar has dissolved.
Bring to the boil, then reduce the heat and
simmer, stirring the sauce occasionally, for
2 minutes. To serve, turn the cakes out onto
serving plates, pierce the tops a few times with
a skewer and drizzle with the sauce.

Bring the dates and water to the boil, then stir in the bicarbonate of soda and butter.

Combine the golden syrup, cream, remaining butter and sugar in a saucepan over low heat.

Sacher squares

PREPARATION TIME: 1 HOUR | TOTAL COOKING TIME: 50 MINUTES | MAKES 24

BASE

60 g (2¼ oz) unsalted butter, chopped
125 g (4½ oz/1 cup) plain (all-purpose) flour
60 g (2¼ oz/¼ cup) sugar
2 egg yolks, lightly beaten
2 teaspoons iced water

CAKE

125 g (4½ oz/1 cup) plain (all-purpose) flour
40 g (1½ oz/⅓ cup) unsweetened cocoa
    powder
250 g (9 oz/1 cup) caster (superfine) sugar
100 g (3½ oz) unsalted butter
2 tablespoons apricot jam
4 eggs, separated
315 g (11 oz/1 cup) apricot jam, extra

TOPPING

185 ml (6 fl oz/¾ cup) cream
250 g (9 oz) dark chocolate, chopped

1 Preheat oven to 180°C (350°F/Gas 4). Cut a 28 x 18 cm (11¼ x 7 inch) rectangle of baking paper. Using fingertips, rub the butter into the sifted flour until fine and crumbly. Stir in the sugar. Add the yolks and most of the water, and mix to a dough, adding more liquid if necessary. Knead until smooth. Roll out and cut to fit the baking paper. Place on a baking tray and bake for 10 minutes or until golden. Leave to cool completely.

2 To make the cake, preheat oven to 180°C (350°F/Gas 4). Grease a 28 x 18 cm (11¼ x 7 inch) shallow tin and line with baking paper. Sift flour and cocoa into a bowl. Combine the sugar, butter and jam in a small pan. Stir over low heat until sugar is dissolved, then add to the dry ingredients. Stir until just combined. Add the yolks and mix well. Place egg whites in a clean, dry bowl. Using electric beaters, beat until soft peaks form. Using a metal spoon, fold into mixture. Pour into the prepared tin and bake for 30 minutes. Leave in the tin for 15 minutes before turning out onto a wire rack to cool.

3 Warm the extra jam over a pan of simmering water and push through a fine sieve. Brush base with 80 g (2¾ oz/¼ cup) of the jam. Place cake on the base. Trim each side, cutting the 'crust' from the cake and base and cut into 24 squares. Brush with jam. Place on a rack, over baking paper, leaving 4 cm (1½ inch) between each.

4 To make the topping, place the cream in a small saucepan and bring to the boil. Pour over the chocolate and stir until melted. Cool slightly. Pour topping over each square and use a flat-bladed knife to cover completely. Put the remaining melted chocolate in a piping bag and pipe an 'S' onto each square.

Brush the base with jam using a pastry brush.

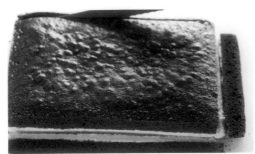
Trim each side, cutting the 'crust' from the cake and base and cut into squares.

Pour chocolate topping over each square and use a flat-bladed knife to cover completely.

Individual white chocolate-chip cakes

PREPARATION TIME: 15 MINUTES I TOTAL COOKING TIME: 20 MINUTES I MAKES 12

110 g (3¾ oz) unsalted butter, softened
185 g (6½ oz/¾ cup) caster (superfine) sugar
2 eggs, lightly beaten
1 teaspoon vanilla essence
290 g (10¼ oz) self-raising flour, sifted
125 ml (4 fl oz/½ cup) buttermilk
250 g (9 oz) white chocolate chips
200 g (7 oz) white chocolate melts (buttons)
12 yellow sugar flowers, to decorate, optional

1 Preheat the oven to 170°C (325°F/Gas 3). Lightly grease a 12-hole 125 ml (4 fl oz/½ cup) muffin tin.

2 Place the butter and sugar in a large mixing bowl. Using electric beaters, beat until pale and creamy. Add the beaten eggs, a little at a time, beating well after each addition. Add the vanilla essence and beat until well combined. Fold in the flour alternately with the buttermilk, then fold in the chocolate chips.

3 Fill each muffin hole three-quarters full with the mixture and bake for 20 minutes, or until a skewer comes out clean when inserted into the centre of each cake. Leave in the tin for 5 minutes before turning out onto a wire rack to cool completely. Use a flat-bladed knife to loosen around the edges of the cakes if they stick.

4 Place the chocolate in a heatproof bowl and sit over a pan with simmering water, making sure the base does not touch the water. Stir until the chocolate has melted. Using a flat-bladed knife, spread chocolate over the cooled muffins and decorate with sugar flowers, if you like. Let set.

Prepare the muffin tin by lightly brushing it with oil or melted butter.

Use a spoon to fold in the flour, buttermilk and chocolate chips.

Leave the cakes to sit in the tin for 5 minutes, then turn out onto a wire rack.

Mini mango cakes with lime syrup

PREPARATION TIME: 25 MINUTES | TOTAL COOKING TIME: 35 MINUTES | MAKES 4

425 g (15 oz) tinned mango slices in syrup,
    drained
90 g (3¼ oz) unsalted butter, softened
185 g (6½ oz/¾ cup) caster (superfine) sugar
2 eggs, lightly beaten
60 g (2¼ oz/½ cup) self-raising flour
2 tablespoons ground almonds
2 tablespoons coconut milk
2 tablespoons lime juice

1   Preheat the oven to 200°C (400°F/Gas 6).
Lightly grease a 4-hole 250 ml (9 fl oz/1 cup)
muffin tin and line with mango slices. Beat the
butter and 125 g (4½ oz/½ cup) of the sugar in a
bowl with electric beaters until light and creamy.
Add the egg, a little at a time, beating well after
each addition. Fold in the sifted flour, add the
almonds and coconut milk, then spoon into the
muffin tin. Bake for 25 minutes, or until a skewer
comes out clean when inserted into the centre of
the cakes.

2   To make the lime syrup, place the lime juice,
the remaining sugar and 125 ml (4 fl oz/½ cup)
water in a small saucepan and stir over low heat
until the sugar is dissolved. Increase the heat and
simmer for 10 minutes. Pierce holes in each cake
with a skewer. Drizzle the syrup over the top
and allow to stand for 5 minutes to soak up the
liquid. Turn out and serve.

Line each muffin hole with mango slices then
spoon in the mixture.

Drizzle the lime syrup over the cakes while still in
the tin. Leave to stand for 5 minutes.

Rum baba with figs

PREPARATION TIME: 40 MINUTES + 2 HOURS STANDING I TOTAL COOKING TIME: 35 MINUTES I SERVES 10

185 g (6½ oz/1½ cups) plain (all-purpose)
  flour
2 teaspoons dried yeast
¼ teaspoon salt
2 teaspoons sugar
80 ml (2½ fl oz/⅓ cup) lukewarm milk
80 g (2¾ oz) unsalted butter
3 eggs, lightly beaten
375 g (13 oz/1½ cups) caster (superfine)
  sugar
80 ml (2½ fl oz/⅓ cup) dark rum
240 g (8½ oz/¾ cup) apricot jam
2 tablespoons dark rum, extra
4–6 figs

1 Lightly brush ten 125 ml (4 fl oz/½ cup) dariole moulds with oil. Place 1 tablespoon of the flour and the yeast, salt, sugar and milk in a small bowl. Cover with plastic wrap and leave in a warm place until foamy. Using fingertips, rub butter into the remaining flour in a large mixing bowl, until it resembles fine breadcrumbs.

2 Add the yeast mixture and eggs to the flour mixture. Beat with a spoon for 2 minutes, until smooth and glossy. Scrape the mixture down the side of the bowl. Cover and leave in a warm place for 1½ hours, until well risen.

3 Preheat the oven to 210°C (415°F/Gas 6–7). Using a wooden spoon, beat the mixture for 2 minutes, then divide between prepared tins. Set aside, covered with plastic wrap, until dough is well risen. Bake for 20 minutes. Meanwhile, combine 500 ml (17 fl oz/2 cups) water and sugar in a pan. Stir over medium heat without boiling until the sugar is dissolved. Bring to the boil then reduce heat and simmer, without stirring, for 15 minutes. Remove from heat, cool slightly and add rum.

4 Turn out onto a wire rack placed over a shallow oven tray. Brush the babas with warm rum syrup until well soaked. Strain excess syrup to remove any crumbs and reserve syrup.

5 Heat the jam in a small saucepan and strain. Add the extra rum, stir to combine and brush over the babas to glaze. Place babas on a serving plate, drizzle the reserved syrup around them. Cut figs in half and serve with the babas.

The yeast mixture will become foamy after sitting in a warm place for 10 minutes.

Pour the mixture into the prepared tins and set aside to allow the dough to rise.

Brush the babas liberally with the rum syrup while they are still warm.

Butterfly cupcakes

PREPARATION TIME: 10 MINUTES | TOTAL COOKING TIME: 30 MINUTES | MAKES 12

125 g (4½ oz) unsalted butter, softened
160 g (5¾ oz/⅔ cup) caster (superfine) sugar
285 g (10 oz) self-raising flour
125 ml (4 fl oz/½ cup) milk
2 eggs
125 ml (4 fl oz/½ cup) thick (double/heavy) cream
80 g (2¾ oz/¼ cup) strawberry jam
icing (confectioners') sugar, to dust

1 Preheat the oven to 180°C (350°F/Gas 4). Line a flat-bottomed 12-hole mini muffin tin with paper cases. Place the butter, sugar, flour, milk and eggs in a large mixing bowl. Using electric beaters, beat on low speed then increase the speed and beat until the mixture is smooth and pale. Divide the mixture evenly among the cases and bake for 30 minutes, or until a skewer inserted into the centre comes out clean. Transfer to a wire rack to cool.

2 Cut shallow rounds from the centre of each cake using the point of a sharp knife, then cut the rounds in half. Spoon 2 teaspoons of cream into each cavity, top with 1 teaspoon of jam and position two halves of the cake tops in the jam to resemble butterfly wings. Dust with icing sugar.

NOTE: *If using foil paper cases instead of the standard paper ones as suggested, the size and number of butterfly cakes may vary.*

Spoon the mixture into paper cases and bake for 30 minutes or until golden.

Cut shallow rounds from the top of each cake, then cut each round in half to form the 'wings'.

Sultana scones

PREPARATION TIME: 20 MINUTES | TOTAL COOKING TIME: 12 MINUTES | MAKES 12

280 g (10 oz/2¼ cups) self-raising flour
pinch of salt
30 g (1 oz) unsalted butter, cut into small
   pieces
90 g (3¼ oz/⅓ cup) caster (superfine) sugar
30 g (1 oz/¼ cup) sultanas (golden raisins) (see
   VARIATION)
1 egg, lightly beaten
170 ml (5½ fl oz/⅔ cup) milk
extra milk, to glaze
unsalted butter, to serve

1   Preheat the oven to 210°C (415°F/Gas 6–7). Lightly grease a baking tray. Sift the flour and salt into a large mixing bowl. Add the butter and rub in lightly with fingertips.

2   Add the sugar and sultanas and stir to combine. Make a well in the centre of the mixture. Add the egg and almost all the milk. Mix quickly, with a flat-bladed knife, to a soft dough, adding more milk if necessary. Turn out onto a lightly floured surface and knead briefly until smooth. Press or roll out to form a round about 2 cm (¾ inch) thick.

3   Cut the dough into rounds using a floured plain 5 cm (2 inch) cutter or cut into squares or diamonds using a floured knife. Place the rounds close together on the prepared tray and brush with extra milk. Bake for 10–12 minutes, or until golden brown. Serve with butter.

VARIATION: *Use any type of dried fruit in this recipe, for example, currants, raisins, or chopped and stoned dates or prunes.*

Add the sugar and sultanas and stir to combine with a wooden spoon.

Strawberry shortcakes

PREPARATION TIME: 20 MINUTES | TOTAL COOKING TIME: 18 MINUTES | MAKES 8

30 g (1 oz) unsalted butter

2 tablespoons caster (superfine) sugar

1 egg

185 g (6½ oz/1½ cups) self-raising flour

pinch of salt

80 ml (2½ fl oz/⅓ cup) milk

1 tablespoon milk, extra

1 tablespoon caster (superfine) sugar, extra

fresh strawberries, hulled and halved, to serve

whipping cream, whipped, to serve

1 Preheat the oven to 210°C (415°F/Gas 6–7). Lightly grease a baking tray. Place the butter and sugar in a mixing bowl. Using electric beaters, beat the butter and sugar until light and fluffy. Add the egg and mix well.

2 Sift the flour and salt into another mixing bowl. Make a well in the centre of the dry ingredients. Add the butter, sugar and egg mixture and almost all of the milk. Using a flat-bladed knife, lightly mix until a soft dough forms, adding more milk if necessary. Knead the dough briefly on a lightly floured surface until smooth. Press out dough to a 2 cm (¾ inch) thickness. Using a floured plain 5 cm (2 inch) cutter, cut 12 rounds from the dough and place on the prepared tray.

3 Brush the rounds with the extra milk and top with a sprinkling of caster sugar. Bake for 15–18 minutes, or until lightly golden. Remove and place on a wire rack. When the shortcakes are cool, split and serve with strawberries and whipped cream.

Cream the butter and sugar with electric beaters, then add the egg.

Press out the dough to 2 cm thick and using a floured circle cutter, cut out rounds from the dough.

Plain scones

PREPARATION TIME: 20 MINUTES | TOTAL COOKING TIME: 12 MINUTES | MAKES 12

250 g (9 oz/2 cups) self-raising flour
pinch of salt, optional (see NOTE)
30 g (1 oz) unsalted butter, cut into small pieces
125 ml (4 fl oz/½ cup) milk
milk, extra, to glaze
jam, to serve
whipped cream, to serve

1 Preheat the oven to 210°C (415°F/Gas 6–7). Lightly grease a baking tray. Sift the flour and salt, if using, into a large mixing bowl. Add the butter and rub in lightly using your fingertips.

2 Make a well in the centre of the flour. Add almost all of the combined milk and 80 ml (2½ fl oz/⅓ cup) water. Mix with a flat-bladed knife to a soft dough, adding more liquid, if necessary.

3 Turn the dough out onto a lightly floured surface (use self-raising flour). Knead the dough briefly and lightly until smooth. Press or roll out the dough to form a round about 1–2 cm (½–¾ inch) thick.

4 Cut the dough into rounds using a floured round 5 cm (2 inch) cutter. Place the rounds on the prepared tray and glaze with the milk. Bake for 10–12 minutes, or until golden brown. Serve with jam and whipped cream.

STORAGE: *Best eaten on the day of making.*

NOTE: *Add a pinch of salt to your scones, even the sweet ones. Salt acts as a flavour enhancer and will not be tasted in the cooked product.*

Mix the mixture with a flat-bladed knife to form a soft dough, adding more liquid if necessary.

Raspberry bun scones

PREPARATION TIME: 20 MINUTES | TOTAL COOKING TIME: 12 MINUTES | MAKES 8

250 g (9 oz/2 cups) self-raising flour
pinch of salt
2 tablespoons caster (superfine) sugar
125 ml (4 fl oz/½ cup) milk
30 g (1 oz) unsalted butter, melted
80 ml (2½ fl oz/⅓ cup) water
1 tablespoon raspberry jam
1 tablespoon milk, extra
caster (superfine) sugar, extra
unsalted butter, to serve

1   Preheat the oven to 210°C (415°F/Gas 6–7).
Lightly grease a baking tray. Sift the flour and
salt into a large mixing bowl. Add the sugar
and stir to combine.

2   Make a well in the centre of the flour. Place
the milk and melted butter in a separate bowl
and combine. Add to the flour mixture all at
once, reserving a teaspoonful for glazing. Add
almost all of the water. Mix quickly, using a flat-
bladed knife, to form a soft dough, adding more
water if necessary.

3   Knead the dough briefly on a lightly floured
surface until smooth. Roll out the dough to a
1 cm (½ inch) thickness, then cut the dough into
8 rounds using a floured 7 cm (2¾ inch) cutter.
Turn each of the scones over and make an
indentation in the centre with your thumb. Place
½ teaspoon of jam in the indentation and fold
over dough. Place the rounds, well apart, on the
prepared tray and flatten tops. Brush with the
milk and sprinkle with the extra caster sugar.
Bake for 10–12 minutes, or until golden. Serve
warm with butter.

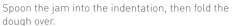
Spoon the jam into the indentation, then fold the
dough over.

Pumpkin scones

PREPARATION TIME: 35 MINUTES | TOTAL COOKING TIME: 12 MINUTES | MAKES 12

30 g (1 oz) unsalted butter, chopped
2 tablespoons caster (superfine) sugar
125 g (4½ oz/½ cup) mashed cooked
    pumpkin (winter squash) (see NOTE)
1 egg, lightly beaten
125 ml (4 fl oz/½ cup) milk
340 g (11¾ oz/2¾ cups) self-raising flour
pinch of salt
milk, to glaze
unsalted butter, to serve

1 Preheat the oven to 210°C (415°F/Gas 6–7). Lightly grease a baking tray. Using electric beaters, beat the butter and sugar in a small mixing bowl until the mixture is light and creamy. Add the pumpkin, egg and milk. Mix until well combined.

2 Sift the flour and salt into a large mixing bowl. Make a well in the centre and add almost all of the mashed pumpkin mixture. Mix lightly, using a flat-bladed knife, to form a soft dough, adding more liquid if necessary.

3 Knead the dough briefly on a lightly floured surface. Roll dough out to 2 cm (¾ inch) thick.

4 Cut into rounds using a floured plain 5 cm (2 inch) cutter. Place the rounds, close together, on the prepared tray and brush with a little milk. Bake for 10–12 minutes, or until golden brown. Serve warm with butter.

NOTE: *To make 125 g (4½ oz/½ cup) of mashed pumpkin you will need around 250 g (9 oz) of raw pumpkin.*

Add the pumpkin, egg and milk to the butter mixture and stir well with a wooden spoon.

Place the rounds, close together, on the prepared tray and brush with a little milk.

Honey, date and ginger scones

PREPARATION TIME: 25 MINUTES I TOTAL COOKING TIME: 15 MINUTES I MAKES 10

90 g (3¼ oz/½ cup) stoned dates
55 g (2 oz/¼ cup) glacé (candied) ginger
250 g (9 oz/2 cups) self-raising flour
½ teaspoon ground ginger
pinch of salt
1 tablespoon honey
125 ml (4 fl oz/½ cup) milk
60 ml (2 fl oz/¼ cup) cream

HONEY GLAZE
1 tablespoon milk
1 teaspoon honey

1   Preheat the oven to 210°C (415°F/Gas 6–7). Lightly grease a baking tray. Chop the dates and the glacé ginger into small chunks. Sift the flour, ground ginger and salt into a mixing bowl. Add the dates and glacé ginger. Stir to combine.

2   Combine the honey, milk and cream in a small saucepan and stir over low heat until combined. Add to the flour and mix lightly, with a flat-bladed knife, to form a soft dough, adding more milk if necessary. (The dough should have just lost its stickiness but not become dried or tough.)

3   Knead the dough briefly on a lightly floured surface until smooth, then press out to 2 cm (¾ inch) thickness. Cut out 10 rounds with a floured plain 5 cm (2 inch) cutter. Place the rounds on the prepared tray and brush with the honey glaze (see Step 4). Cook for 12–15 minutes, or until lightly golden.

4   To make the honey glaze, gently warm the milk and honey in a saucepan, stirring constantly until well combined.

NOTE: *Use self-raising flour on your hands and work surfaces.*

Chop the dates and glacé ginger into small chunks.

Add the cream mixture to the flour and mix lightly, with a flat-bladed knife, to form a soft dough.

Wholemeal date scones

PREPARATION TIME: 20 MINUTES | TOTAL COOKING TIME: 20 MINUTES | MAKES 12

185 g (6½ oz/1½ cups) self-raising flour
225 g (8 oz/1½ cups) wholemeal (whole-wheat)
    self-raising flour
½ teaspoon baking powder
¼ teaspoon salt
60 g (2¼ oz) unsalted butter, cut into small
    pieces
2 tablespoons caster (superfine) sugar
185 g (6½ oz) stoned dates, chopped
315 ml (10¾ fl oz/1¼ cups) buttermilk
125 ml (4 fl oz/½ cup) water
buttermilk, extra, to glaze
butter or whipped cream, to serve, optional

1   Preheat the oven to 210°C (415°F/Gas 6–7).
Lightly grease a baking tray. Sift the flours,
baking powder and salt into a large mixing bowl,
returning the husks to the bowl. Add the butter
and rub in lightly using your fingertips. Stir in
the sugar and the dates.

2   Make a well in the centre of the flour
mixture. Add the buttermilk and almost all
of the water. Mix quickly, using a flat-bladed
knife, to form a soft dough, adding more water
if necessary. (The dough should have lost its
stickiness but not become too dry or tough.)

3   Knead dough briefly on a lightly floured
surface until smooth. Press out the dough with
floured hands to form a 2 cm (¾ inch) thick
square. Cut into 12 smaller squares. Place the
squares on the prepared tray, leaving a 2 cm
(¾ inch) gap between each scone. Brush with
extra buttermilk.

4   Bake the scones for 18–20 minutes, or until
golden brown. Serve straight from the oven with
butter or whipped cream, if desired.

NOTE: *These scones are more heavily textured
than the traditional recipe. Returning the flour
husks to the mixture will contribute to this texture,
however it is still necessary to sift the flours as this
introduces air through the dry ingredients.*

Sift the self-raising flours into a large mixing bowl, returning the husks.

Place the dough squares on the prepared tray, making sure they are well spaced.

Cinnamon scrolls

PREPARATION TIME: 25 MINUTES | TOTAL COOKING TIME: 12 MINUTES | MAKES 12

250 g (9 oz/2 cups) self-raising flour
pinch of salt
90 g (3¼ oz) unsalted butter, chopped
170 ml (5½ fl oz/⅔ cup) milk

FILLING
60 g (2¼ oz) unsalted butter, softened
2 tablespoons soft brown sugar
1 teaspoon ground cinnamon

ICING
60 g (2¼ oz/½ cup) icing (confectioners')
    sugar, sifted
2 teaspoons boiling water

1   Preheat the oven to 210°C (415°F/Gas 6–7). Lightly grease a baking tray. Sift the flour and salt into a mixing bowl. Using fingertips, rub the butter into the flour. Make a well in the centre and add almost all the milk. Mix lightly, with a flat-bladed knife, until a soft dough forms, adding more liquid if necessary. Knead the dough briefly on a lightly floured surface until smooth. Roll out to a 40 x 25 cm (16 x 10 inch) rectangle of 5 mm (¼ inch) thickness.

2   To make the filling, place all the ingredients in a mixing bowl. Using electric beaters, beat until light and fluffy. Spread the filling evenly over the dough rectangle and roll up from the long side. Using a sharp knife, slice the dough into twelve 3 cm (1¼ inch) pieces. Place the dough pieces close together, cut side up, on the prepared tray. Bake for 12 minutes, or until golden brown. Remove from the oven and leave to cool slightly. Drizzle the icing (see Step 3) over the top.

3   To make the icing (frosting), combine the icing sugar and boiling water in a small mixing bowl. Beat the mixture until smooth and well combined.

VARIATION: *Add chopped sultanas (golden raisins) to the filling, if desired.*

Using a flat-bladed knife, spread the filling evenly over the dough rectangle.

Place the scrolls, close together, on the prepared tray and bake until golden brown.

Muffins

Double choc muffins

PREPARATION TIME: 25 MINUTES I TOTAL COOKING TIME: 12–15 MINUTES I MAKES 6 LARGE MUFFINS

250 g (9 oz/2 cups) plain (all-purpose) flour
2½ teaspoons baking powder
30 g (1 oz/¼ cup) unsweetened cocoa powder
2 tablespoons caster (superfine) sugar
130 g (4½ oz) dark chocolate chips
1 egg, lightly beaten
125 g (4½ oz/½ cup) sour cream
185 ml (6 fl oz/¾ cup) milk
90 g (3¼ oz) unsalted butter, melted

TOPPING
50 g (1¾ oz) dark chocolate, chopped
1 tablespoon cream
10 g (¼ oz) butter

1 Preheat the oven to 180°C (350°F/Gas 4). Brush a 6-hole large muffin tin with melted butter or oil. Sift the flour, baking powder and cocoa into a large mixing bowl. Add the sugar and the chocolate chips and mix. Make a well in the centre.

2 Add the combined egg, sour cream, milk and melted butter all at once and stir with a fork until just combined. (Do not overbeat as the batter should look quite lumpy.)

3 Spoon the batter into the prepared muffin holes. Bake for 12–15 minutes, or until firm. Loosen muffins with a flat-bladed knife and turn out onto a wire rack to cool completely.

4 Combine the chocolate, cream and butter in a pan. Stir over low heat until smooth. Refrigerate until firm but not set. Spread the topping over the muffins using a flat-bladed knife, or put it in a piping (icing) bag with a large fluted piping tip and pipe the chocolate topping on top of the muffins.

Make a well in the flour mixture and fold in the combined butter, eggs and milk.

The muffins can be topped with a chocolate and cream mixture.

Baby coffee and walnut sour cream muffins

PREPARATION TIME: 15 MINUTES I TOTAL COOKING TIME: 20 MINUTES I MAKES 24

75 g (2½ oz) walnuts
155 g (5½ oz/⅔ cup) firmly packed soft brown
    sugar
125 g (4½ oz) unsalted butter, softened
2 eggs, lightly beaten
125 g (4½ oz/1 cup) self-raising flour
80 g (2¾ oz/⅓ cup) sour cream
1 tablespoon coffee and chicory essence

1 Preheat the oven to 160°C (315°F/Gas 2–3).
Lightly grease two 12-hole 30 ml (1 fl oz) baby
muffin tins. Process the walnuts and 45 g
(1½ oz/¼ cup) of the brown sugar in a food
processor until the walnuts are roughly chopped
into small pieces. Transfer to a mixing bowl.

2 Cream the butter and remaining sugar
together in the food processor until pale and
creamy. With the motor running, gradually add
the egg and process until smooth. Add the flour
and blend until well mixed. Add the sour cream
and essence and process until thoroughly mixed.

3 Spoon ½ teaspoon of the walnut and sugar
mixture into the base of each muffin hole,
followed by a heaped teaspoon of the cake
mixture. Sprinkle a little more walnut mixture
over the top, add another heaped teaspoon of the
cake mixture and top with the remaining walnut
mixture. Bake for 20 minutes, or until risen
and springy to the touch. Leave in the tins for
5 minutes. Remove the cakes using a flat-bladed
knife to loosen the side and base, then transfer to
a wire rack to cool completely.

Process the walnuts and brown sugar in a food
processor until the walnuts are roughly chopped.

Process the remaining ingredients until smooth and
thoroughly combined.

Layer walnut and cake mixtures in the muffin holes,
finishing with a layer of the walnut mixture.

Orange poppy seed muffins

PREPARATION TIME: 20 MINUTES I TOTAL COOKING TIME: 12 MINUTES I SERVES 12

215 g (7½ oz/1¾ cups) self-raising flour
1 tablespoon caster (superfine) sugar
1 teaspoon baking powder
¼ teaspoon bicarbonate of soda (baking soda)
1 tablespoon poppy seeds
90 g (3¼ oz) unsalted butter
160 g (5½ oz/½ cup) orange marmalade
1 egg, lightly beaten
185 ml (6 fl oz/¾ cup) milk

1   Preheat the oven to 210°C (415°F/ Gas 6–7). Lightly grease a 12-hole muffin tin. Sift the flour, sugar, baking powder and bicarbonate of soda into a mixing bowl. Add the poppy seeds and stir. Make a well in the centre.

2   Combine the butter and marmalade in a small saucepan and stir over low heat until the marmalade becomes runny and the butter has melted. Add the butter mixture and combined egg and milk to the flour mixture, and stir until just combined. (Do not overmix as the batter should be quite lumpy.)

3   Spoon the batter into the prepared muffin holes and cook for 10–12 minutes or until golden. Loosen the muffins with a flat-bladed knife and transfer to a wire rack.

VARIATION: *Beat 60 g (2¼ oz) soft butter, 2 tablespoons icing (confectioners') sugar and 1 teaspoon grated orange zest until light and creamy. Cut a small section from the top of the muffin, fill with mixture and replace the tops.*

Add the butter mixture and combined egg and milk to the flour mixture.

Spoon the batter into the prepared tin and cook for 10–12 minutes or until golden.

Plain muffins

PREPARATION TIME: 15 MINUTES | TOTAL COOKING TIME: 25 MINUTES | MAKES 12

310 g (11 oz/2½ cups) self-raising flour
60 g (2¼ oz/¼ cup) caster (superfine) sugar
2 teaspoons baking powder
2 eggs, lightly beaten
310 ml (10¾ fl oz/1¼ cups) milk
160 g (5½ oz) unsalted butter, melted

1   Preheat the oven to 210°C (415°F/Gas 6–7). Lightly grease a 12-hole muffin tin.

2   Sift the flour, sugar and baking powder into a large mixing bowl. Make a well in the centre.

3   Place the egg, milk and butter in a separate mixing bowl. Combine and add all at once to the flour mixture. Stir gently with a fork or rubber spatula until the mixture is just moistened. (Do not overmix as the batter should look quite lumpy.)

4   Spoon the mixture evenly into the prepared muffin holes until two-thirds full. Bake for 20–25 minutes, or until golden brown. Loosen the muffins with a flat-bladed knife and transfer to a wire rack to cool.

VARIATION: *Beat 80 ml (2½ fl oz/⅓ cup) whipping cream together with 1 tablespoon icing (confectioners') sugar until soft peaks form. Cut a circle from the top of each muffin, about 2 cm (¾ inch) deep, and cut these circles in half to make 'wings'. Spoon ½ teaspoon strawberry jam into each muffin, top with the cream mixture and arrange the 'wings' in the cream.*

Sift the flour and baking powder into a large mixing bowl.

Spoon the mixture evenly into the prepared muffin holes and bake until golden brown.

Blueberry muffins

PREPARATION TIME: 20 MINUTES | TOTAL COOKING TIME: 20 MINUTES | MAKES 12

375 g (13 oz/3 cups) plain (all-purpose) flour
1 tablespoon baking powder
165 g (5¾ oz/¾ cup) firmly packed soft brown
    sugar
125 g (4½ oz) unsalted butter, melted
2 eggs, lightly beaten
250 ml (9 fl oz/1 cup) milk
185 g (6½ oz) fresh or thawed frozen
    blueberries

1 Preheat the oven to 210°C (415°F/Gas 6–7).
Lightly grease two 6-hole muffin tins. Sift the
flour and baking powder into a large mixing
bowl. Stir in the sugar and make a well in the
centre of the dry ingredients.

2 In a separate mixing bowl, add the melted
butter, eggs and milk and stir to combine. Add
all at once to the flour mixture and fold until just
combined. (Do not overmix as the batter should
look quite lumpy.)

3 Fold in the blueberries. Spoon the batter into
the prepared muffin holes. Bake for 20 minutes,
or until golden brown. Turn out onto a wire rack
to cool.

Make a well in the flour mixture and fold in the
combined butter, eggs and milk.

Lightly fold the blueberries into the mixture, making
sure they are well incorporated.

Spoon the batter into the prepared muffin tins and
bake until golden brown.

White chocolate mango muffins

PREPARATION TIME: 10 MINUTES | TOTAL COOKING TIME: 20 MINUTES | MAKES 12

340 g (11¾ oz/2¾ cups) self-raising flour
95 g (3¼ oz/½ cup) soft brown sugar
130 g (4½ oz) chopped white chocolate
185 g (6½ oz/1 cup) chopped fresh mango
    flesh (2 medium) or 440 g (15½ oz)
    tinned mango pieces, well drained
125 ml (4 fl oz/½ cup) milk
60 ml (2 fl oz/¼ cup) cream
90 g (3¼ oz) unsalted butter, melted
1 egg, lightly beaten

1   Preheat the oven to 180°C (350°F/Gas 4). Fill a 12-hole muffin tin with paper cases. Sift the flour into a large mixing bowl. Stir in the sugar and chopped chocolate and mix well. Fold in the chopped mango gently. Make a well in the centre of the mixture.

2   Add the combined milk, cream, butter and egg all at once. Mix with a fork or rubber spatula until just combined. (Do not overmix as the batter should look quite lumpy.) Spoon the mixture into the paper cases.

3   Bake for 20 minutes, or until lightly golden. Loosen the muffins with a flat-bladed knife and turn out onto a wire rack to cool completely.

NOTE: *Serve these muffins warm with whipped cream. They also make an unusual, but delicious, dessert, topped with large shavings of white chocolate or served split with stewed apples.*

Stir in the sugar and chopped white chocolate and mix well.

Mix with a fork or rubber spatula until just combined (the batter should look quite lumpy).

Banana muffins

PREPARATION TIME: 15 MINUTES | TOTAL COOKING TIME: 15 MINUTES | MAKES 12

250 g (9 oz/2 cups) self-raising flour
75 g (2½ oz/1 cup) oat bran
185 g (6½ oz/¾ cup) caster (superfine) sugar
60 g (2¼ oz) unsalted butter, melted
170 ml (5½ fl oz/⅔ cup) milk
2 eggs, lightly beaten
2 ripe medium bananas, mashed

1   Preheat the oven to 210°C (415°F/Gas 6–7). Lightly grease a 12-hole muffin tin. Sift the flour into a large bowl and add the oat bran and sugar. Make a well in the centre of the dry ingredients.

2   Combine the butter, milk, eggs and banana in a separate mixing bowl and add to the flour mixture all at once. Using a wooden spoon, stir until just mixed. (Do not overbeat as the batter should remain lumpy.)

3   Spoon the mixture into the prepared muffin holes. Bake for 15 minutes, or until puffed and golden brown. Transfer the muffins to a wire rack to cool.

VARIATION: *For muffins with a difference, beat 100 g (3½ oz) cream cheese, 2 tablespoons icing (confectioners') sugar and 2 teaspoons lemon juice with electric beaters until light and creamy. Spread over the muffins and top with dried banana slices.*

Make a well in the centre of the dry ingredients and pour in the liquid ingredients.

Muesli muffins

PREPARATION TIME: 15 MINUTES + 20 MINUTES STANDING I TOTAL COOKING TIME: 25 MINUTES I MAKES 6 LARGE MUFFINS

95 g (3¼ oz) dried apricots, chopped
125 ml (4 fl oz/½ cup) orange juice
2 teaspoons finely grated orange zest
150 g (5½ oz/1 cup) wholemeal (whole-wheat)
    self-raising flour
60 g (2¼ oz/½ cup) self-raising flour
½ teaspoon baking powder
45 g (1½ oz/¼ cup) lightly packed soft brown
    sugar
75 g (2½ oz) toasted muesli (granola)
185 ml (6 fl oz/¾ cup) milk
60 g (2¼ oz) unsalted butter, melted

TOPPING
1 tablespoon plain (all-purpose) flour
½ teaspoon ground cinnamon
45 g (1½ oz/¼ cup) lightly packed soft brown
    sugar
35 g (1¼ oz) toasted muesli (granola)
20 g (¾ oz) unsalted butter, melted

1   Preheat the oven to 210°C (415°F/Gas 6–7).
Lightly grease a 6-hole large muffin tin. Combine
the apricots, orange juice and zest in a mixing
bowl. Set the mixture aside for 20 minutes.

2   Sift the flours and baking powder into a large
mixing bowl. Add the brown sugar and muesli
and stir through.

3   Add the combined milk, butter and undrained
apricot mixture. Mix quickly with a fork until all
ingredients are just moistened. Spoon the mixture
evenly into the prepared muffin holes.

4   To make the topping, place all ingredients in
a bowl and stir to combine. Sprinkle the topping
over the muffins.

5   Bake the muffins for 20–25 minutes, or until
golden brown. Loosen muffins with a flat-bladed
knife and turn out onto a wire rack to cool
completely. Serve with butter, if desired.

STORAGE: *These muffins can be frozen for up to*
3 months. Reheat in a 180°C (350°F/Gas 4) oven
for 10 minutes.

Add the brown sugar and muesli to the dry
ingredients and stir through.

Spoon the topping over the tops of the muffins
before baking for 20–25 minutes.

Berry cheesecake muffins

PREPARATION TIME: 15 MINUTES | TOTAL COOKING TIME: 30 MINUTES | MAKES 6 LARGE MUFFINS

215 g (7½ oz/1¾ cups) self-raising flour
2 eggs, lightly beaten
60 ml (2 fl oz/¼ cup) vegetable oil
2 tablespoons raspberry jam
60 g (2¼ oz/¼ cup) mixed berry yoghurt
125 g (4½ oz/½ cup) caster (superfine) sugar
50 g (1¾ oz) cream cheese (see NOTE)
1 tablespoon raspberry jam, extra, for filling
icing (confectioners') sugar, sifted, to dust

1 Preheat the oven to 180°C (350°F/Gas 4). Lightly grease a 6-hole muffin tin. Sift the flour into a large mixing bowl and make a well in the centre. Place the eggs, oil, jam, yoghurt and sugar in a separate bowl and combine. Add all at once to the sifted flour. Mix the batter until just combined. (Do not overmix as the batter should look quite lumpy.)

2 Spoon three-quarters of the mixture into the prepared muffin holes. Cut the cream cheese into six equal portions and place a portion on the centre of each muffin. Spread tops with jam and cover with the remaining muffin batter.

3 Bake for 25–30 minutes, or until the muffins are golden. Loosen the muffins with a flat-bladed knife then turn out onto a wire rack to cool completely. Dust with icing sugar.

NOTE: *These muffins are best eaten as soon as they are cool enough. The cream cheese filling will melt slightly as the muffins cook and provide a delicious 'surprise' centre.*

Mix the batter until just combined. Do not overmix as the batter should look quite lumpy.

Place a portion of cream cheese in the centre of each muffin.

Strawberry and passionfruit muffins

PREPARATION TIME: 20 MINUTES | TOTAL COOKING TIME: 15 MINUTES | MAKES 12

215 g (7½ oz/1¾ cups) self-raising flour
pinch of salt
1 teaspoon baking powder
½ teaspoon bicarbonate of soda (baking soda)
60 g (2¼ oz/¼ cup) caster (superfine) sugar
175 g (6 oz/1 cup) fresh strawberries, hulled
   and chopped
1 egg
185 ml (6 fl oz/¾ cup) milk
125 g (4½ oz/½ cup) passionfruit pulp, tinned
   or fresh
60 g (2¼ oz) unsalted butter, melted
whipping cream, whipped, to serve
fresh strawberries, hulled and halved, extra
icing (confectioners') sugar, to dust (optional)

1 Preheat the oven to 210°C (415°F/Gas 6–7).
Lightly grease a 12-hole muffin tin.

2 Sift the flour, salt, baking powder,
bicarbonate of soda and sugar into a mixing
bowl. Add the strawberries and stir to combine.
Make a well in the centre.

3 Place the egg and milk in a separate mixing
bowl and stir to combine. Add the passionfruit
pulp and egg mixture to the flour mixture. Pour
the melted butter all at once and lightly stir with
a fork until just combined. (Do not overmix as
the batter should look quite lumpy.)

4 Spoon the mixture into the prepared muffin
holes and bake for 10–15 minutes, or until
golden brown. Loosen muffins with a flat-bladed
knife and turn out onto a wire rack to cool. Top
with whipped cream and fresh strawberry halves
and sprinkle with icing sugar, if desired.

NOTE: *Folding the fruit through the dry mixture
helps it to be evenly distributed throughout.*

Add the strawberries to the dry ingredients and stir
to combine.

Pour the melted butter into the mixture all at once
and lightly stir with a fork until just combined.

Coffee pecan streusel muffins

PREPARATION TIME: 20 MINUTES | TOTAL COOKING TIME: 12 MINUTES | MAKES 9

215 g (7½ oz/1¾ cups) self-raising flour
1 teaspoon baking powder
60 g (2¼ oz/¼ cup) caster (superfine) sugar
60 g (2¼ oz/½ cup) finely chopped pecans
1 tablespoon instant coffee
1 tablespoon boiling water
1 egg
170 ml (5½ fl oz/⅔ cup) milk
80 ml (2½ fl oz/⅓ cup) vegetable oil
icing (confectioners') sugar, to dust (optional)

STREUSEL TOPPING
30 g (1 oz/¼ cup) self-raising flour
30 g (1 oz) unsalted butter
2 tablespoons soft brown sugar
1 teaspoon ground cinnamon
2 tablespoons finely chopped pecans

1 Preheat the oven to 210°C (415°F/Gas 6–7).
Lightly grease nine holes of a 12-hole muffin tin.
Sift the flour and baking powder into a mixing
bowl. Add the sugar and pecans. Make a well in
the centre.

2 Combine the instant coffee with the boiling
water and stir until dissolved. Cool and add to
the flour mixture. In a separate bowl, combine
the egg, milk and oil. Add to the flour mixture
and stir until just combined. (Do not overmix as
the batter should look quite lumpy.)

3 To make the topping, place the flour into a
mixing bowl. Rub the butter into the flour until
the mixture resembles coarse breadcrumbs. Add
the sugar, cinnamon and pecans and mix until
well combined.

4 Spoon the muffin mixture into the prepared
muffin holes. Sprinkle with the topping and
bake for 10–12 minutes, or until golden brown.
Loosen the muffins with a flat-bladed knife and
turn out onto a wire rack to cool completely.
Sprinkle with icing sugar, if desired.

Add the sugar, cinnamon and pecans to the
topping mixture.

Cakes

Chocolate mud cake

PREPARATION TIME: 30 MINUTES I TOTAL COOKING TIME: 1 HOUR 30 MINUTES I SERVES 8–10

250 g (9 oz) unsalted butter

250 g (9 oz) dark chocolate, chopped

2 tablespoons instant coffee

185 ml (6 fl oz/¾ cup) hot water

150 g (5½ oz/1¼ cups) self-raising flour

150 g (5½ oz/1¼ cups) plain (all-purpose) flour

½ teaspoon bicarbonate of soda (baking soda)

60 g (2¼ oz/½ cup) unsweetened cocoa powder

550 g (1 lb 4 oz/2¼ cups) caster (superfine) sugar

4 eggs, lightly beaten

2 tablespoons vegetable oil

125 ml (4 fl oz/½ cup) buttermilk

ICING

150 g (5½ oz) unsalted butter, chopped

150 g (5½ oz) dark chocolate, chopped

1 Preheat the oven to 160°C (315°F/Gas 2–3). Lightly grease a deep 22 cm (8½ inch) round cake tin and line with baking paper, making sure the paper around the side extends at least 5 cm (2 inches) above the top edge.

2 Put the butter, chocolate, coffee and water in a saucepan and stir over low heat until smooth. Remove from the heat.

3 Sift the flours, bicarbonate of soda and cocoa into a large mixing bowl. Stir in the sugar and make a well in the centre. Place the eggs, oil and buttermilk in a separate mixing bowl and mix until combined. Pour into the dry ingredients and mix together with a whisk. Gradually add the chocolate mixture, a little at a time, whisking well after each addition.

4 Pour the mixture (it will be quite wet) into the prepared tin and bake for 1¼ hours. Test the centre with a skewer—the skewer may be slightly wetter than normal. Remove the cake from the oven. If the top looks raw, bake for another 5–10 minutes, then remove. Leave in the tin until cold, then turn out and wrap in plastic wrap.

5 For the icing (frosting), combine the butter and chocolate in a saucepan and stir over low heat until the butter and chocolate are melted. Remove and cool slightly. Pour over the cake and allow it to run down the side.

STORAGE: *Keep in the fridge in an airtight container for 3 weeks or in a cool dry place for 1 week. Can be frozen for up to 2 months.*

Stir the butter, chocolate, coffee and water until melted and smooth.

Gradually whisk the chocolate mixture into the well in the dry ingredients.

Pour the cooled chocolate icing over the upside down cake.

Classic sponge

PREPARATION TIME: 20 MINUTES | TOTAL COOKING TIME: 25 MINUTES | SERVES 8

75 g (2½ oz/½ cup) plain (all-purpose) flour
150 g (5½ oz/1¼ cups) self-raising flour
6 eggs
220 g (7¾ oz/1 cup) caster (superfine) sugar
2 tablespoons boiling water
whipping cream, whipped, optional
jam, for filling, optional

1 Preheat the oven to 180°C (350°F/Gas 4). Lightly grease two deep 22 cm (8½ inch) round cake tins and line the bases with baking paper. Dust the tins lightly with a little extra flour, shaking off the excess.

2 Sift the flours three times onto baking paper. Beat the eggs in a large mixing bowl with electric beaters for 7 minutes, or until thick and pale.

3 Gradually add the sugar to the eggs, beating well after each addition. Using a metal spoon, fold in the sifted flour and boiling water. Spread evenly into the prepared tins and bake for 25 minutes, or until each sponge is lightly golden and shrinks slightly from the side of the tin. Leave the sponges in their tins for 5 minutes before turning out onto a wire rack to cool. Slice cake in half and fill with whipped cream and jam, if desired.

STORAGE: *This sponge is best eaten on the day it is made. It won't keep well as it only contains a very small amount of fat. Unfilled sponges can be frozen for up to 1 month—make sure you freeze the cakes in separate freezer bags. Thaw at room temperature for about 20 minutes.*

NOTES: *The secret to making the perfect sponge lies in the folding technique. A beating action, or using a wooden spoon, will cause loss of volume in the egg mixture and result in a flat, heavy cake.*

Another very important factor is the amount of air incorporated in the flour. To make a light-textured sponge, you must sift the flour several times. Sifting not only removes any lumps in the flour but incorporates air.

Take the eggs out of the fridge at least an hour before required so they are at room temperature before adding them to the mixture.

Sift the flours three times onto baking paper.

Using a metal spoon, fold in the flour and hot water.

Butter cake

PREPARATION TIME: 20 MINUTES | TOTAL COOKING TIME: 1 HOUR 15 MINUTES | SERVES 8

280 g (10 oz) unsalted butter
225 g (8 oz/1 cup) caster (superfine) sugar
1½ teaspoons vanilla essence
4 eggs
225 g (8 oz/1¾ cups) self-raising flour
150 g (5½ oz/1¼ cups) plain (all-purpose)
   flour
185 ml (6 fl oz/¾ cup) milk

1   Preheat the oven to 180°C (350°F/Gas 4).
Lightly grease a deep 20 cm (8 inch) round cake
tin and line with baking paper.

2   Place the butter and sugar in a mixing bowl
and beat with electric beaters until light and
creamy. Add the vanilla then the eggs, one at a
time, beating well after each addition.

3   Sift the flours together into a mixing bowl.
Using a large metal spoon, add the combined
flours alternately with the milk into the butter
mixture, folding until smooth. Spoon into the
prepared tin and smooth the surface. Bake for
1¼ hours, or until a skewer comes out clean
when inserted into the centre of the cake.

4   Leave the cake in the tin for 5 minutes before
turning out onto a wire rack to cool completely.

STORAGE: *This butter cake can be kept in an
airtight container in the fridge for up to 1 week,
or for 3–4 days in an airtight container in a cool
dry place. It can be frozen for up to 2 months.*

VARIATIONS: *To make a 22 cm (8½ inch) round
cake, bake for 1 hour 5 minutes. To make a
20 cm (8 inch) square cake, bake for 55 minutes.
To make a 23 cm (9 inch) square cake, bake for
55 minutes.*

Place the butter and sugar in a mixing bowl and
beat until light and creamy.

Spoon the mixture into the prepared tin and
smooth the surface.

Angel food cake with chocolate sauce

PREPARATION TIME: 15 MINUTES | TOTAL COOKING TIME: 45 MINUTES | SERVES 8–10

125 g (4½ oz/1 cup) plain (all-purpose) flour
250 g (9 oz/1 cup) caster (superfine) sugar
10 egg whites, at room temperature
1 teaspoon cream of tartar
¼ teaspoon salt
½ teaspoon vanilla essence

CHOCOLATE SAUCE
250 g (9 oz) dark chocolate, chopped
185 ml (6 fl oz/¾ cup) cream
50 g (1¾ oz) unsalted butter, chopped

1 Preheat the oven to 180°C (350°F/Gas 4). Sift the flour and half the sugar four times into a large mixing bowl. Set aside. Beat the egg whites, cream of tartar and salt in a clean, dry large mixing bowl with electric beaters until soft peaks form. Gradually add the remaining sugar and beat until thick and glossy.

2 Add the vanilla. Sift half the flour and sugar mixture over the meringue mixture and gently fold in with a metal spoon. Repeat with the remaining flour and sugar. Spoon into an ungreased angel cake tin and bake for 45 minutes, or until a skewer comes out clean when inserted into the centre of the cake. Gently loosen around the side of the cake with a spatula, then turn the cake out onto a wire rack to cool completely.

3 To make the chocolate sauce, place the chocolate, cream and butter in a saucepan. Stir over low heat until the chocolate has melted and the mixture is smooth. Drizzle over the cake and serve.

NOTE: *The tin must be very clean and not greased or the cake will not rise and will slip down the side of the tin.*

Using electric beaters, beat the egg whites, cream of tartar and salt until soft peaks form.

Spoon the mixture into an ungreased tin then bake for 45 minutes.

Stir the chocolate, cream and butter over low heat until melted.

Genoise sponge

PREPARATION TIME: 20 MINUTES | TOTAL COOKING TIME: 25 MINUTES | SERVES 8

290 g (10¼ oz/2⅓ cups) plain (all-purpose)
   flour
8 eggs
220 g (7¾ oz) caster (superfine) sugar
100 g (3½ oz) unsalted butter, melted
125ml (4 fl oz/½ cup) whipped cream
raspberries, for filling
icing (confectioners') sugar, (optional)

1   Preheat the oven to 180°C (350°F/Gas 4).
Brush two 22 cm (8½ inch) round cake tins with
melted butter. Line the bases with baking paper,
then grease the paper. Dust the tins lightly with a
little extra flour, shaking off the excess.

2   Sift the flour three times onto baking paper.
Mix the eggs and sugar in a large heatproof bowl.
Place the bowl over a pan of simmering water,
making sure the base doesn't touch the water,
and beat with electric beaters until the mixture is
thick and fluffy and a ribbon of mixture drawn
in a figure of eight doesn't sink immediately.
Remove from the heat and beat for 3 minutes,
or until slightly cooled.

3   Add the cooled butter and sifted flour. Using
a large metal spoon, fold in quickly and lightly
until the mixture is just combined.

4   Spread the mixture evenly into the prepared
tins. Bake for 25 minutes, or until each sponge is
lightly golden and shrinks slightly away from the
side of the tin. Leave the cakes in their tins for
5 minutes before turning out onto a wire rack
to cool. Slice the cake in half and fill with
raspberries and whipped cream. Lightly dust
with icing sugar just before serving, if desired.

NOTE: *The Genoise sponge is traditionally made
in a tin with sloping sides and served dusted with
icing (confectioners') sugar. However, it is often
made as a decorated gateau or celebration cake, in
which case it is generally baked in two sandwich
tins. In this case, ensure you have exactly half the
mixture in each tin by weighing each one first,
then dividing the mixture between the tins before
weighing the tins again to make sure they are equal.*

Dust the tins lightly with a little extra flour, shaking
off any excess.

Beat the mixture until light and fluffy and a ribbon
drawn in a figure of eight doesn't sink immediately.

Chocolate cake

PREPARATION TIME: 25 MINUTES | TOTAL COOKING TIME: 1 HOUR 15 MINUTES | SERVES 10

185 g (6½ oz) unsalted butter

330 g (11½ oz) caster (superfine) sugar

2½ teaspoons vanilla essence

3 eggs

75 g (2½ oz) self-raising flour, sifted

225 g (8 oz) plain (all-purpose) flour, sifted

1½ teaspoons bicarbonate of soda (baking soda)

90 g (3¼ oz/¾ cup) unsweetened cocoa powder

280 ml (9½ fl oz) buttermilk

125 ml (4 fl oz/½ cup) whipped cream

50 g (1¾ oz) almond flakes, roasted

ICING

150 g (5½ oz) unsalted butter, chopped

150 g (5½ oz) dark chocolate, chopped

1   Preheat the oven to 180°C (350°F/Gas 4). Lightly grease a deep, 20 cm (8 inch) round cake tin and line the base with baking paper.

2   Beat the butter and sugar with electric beaters until light and creamy. Beat in the vanilla. Add the eggs, one at a time, beating well after each addition.

3   Using a metal spoon, fold in the combined sifted flours, bicarbonate of soda and cocoa alternately with the buttermilk. Stir until the mixture is just smooth.

4   Spoon the mixture into the prepared tin and smooth the surface. Bake for 1 hour 15 minutes, or until a skewer comes out clean when inserted into the centre of the cake. Leave the cake to cool in the tin for at least 5 minutes before turning out onto a wire rack to cool completely. Cut the cake in half horizontally and fill with the whipped cream.

5   For the icing (frosting), combine the butter and chocolate in a saucepan and stir over low heat until the butter and chocolate are melted. Remove and cool slightly. Pour over the cake and allow it to run down the side. While the icing is still soft sprinkle with the almond flakes.

Using a metal spoon fold in the dry ingredients alternately with the buttermilk.

Spoon the mixture into the prepared tin and smooth the surface.

Devil's food cake

PREPARATION TIME: 15 MINUTES | TOTAL COOKING TIME: 50 MINUTES | SERVES 8–10

165 g (5¾ oz/1⅓ cups) plain (all-purpose) flour
85 g (3 oz/⅔ cup) unsweetened cocoa powder
1 teaspoon bicarbonate of soda (baking soda)
250 g (9 oz/1 cup) sugar
250 ml (9 fl oz/1 cup) buttermilk
2 eggs, lightly beaten
125 g (4½ oz) unsalted butter, softened
125 ml (4 fl oz/½ cup) whipped cream
icing (confectioners') sugar, to dust
250 g (9 oz) fresh berries, to serve (optional)

1 Preheat the oven to 180°C (350°F/Gas 4). Lightly grease a deep 20 cm (8 inch) round cake tin and line the base with baking paper. Sift the flour, cocoa and bicarbonate of soda into a large bowl.

2 Add the sugar to the bowl. Combine the buttermilk, eggs and butter in a separate bowl, then pour onto the dry ingredients. Using electric beaters, beat on low speed for 3 minutes, or until just combined. Increase the speed to high and beat for another 3 minutes, or until the mixture is free of any lumps and increased in volume.

3 Spoon the mixture into the prepared tin and smooth the surface. Bake for 40–50 minutes, or until a skewer comes out clean when inserted into the centre of the cake. Leave the cake in the tin for at least 15 minutes before turning out onto a wire rack to cool completely. Cut the cake in half horizontally and fill with the whipped cream. Dust with icing sugar and serve with fresh berries.

STORAGE: *Unfilled, the cake will keep for 3 days in an airtight container or up to 3 months in the freezer.*

Sifting the dry ingredients aerates them and eliminates any lumps.

Start with the electric beaters on low speed then increase to high after a few minutes.

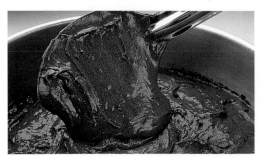

Spoon the mixture into the tin and smooth the surface to ensure your cake has an even top.

Madeira cake

PREPARATION TIME: 10 MINUTES | TOTAL COOKING TIME: 50 MINUTES | SERVES 6

180 g (6 oz) unsalted butter, softened
185 g (6½ oz/¾ cup) caster (superfine) sugar
3 eggs, beaten
155 g (5½ oz/1¼ cups) self-raising flour, sifted
125 g (4½ oz/1 cup) plain (all-purpose) flour, sifted
2 teaspoons finely grated lemon zest
2 tablespoons milk
2 teaspoons caster (superfine) sugar, to sprinkle
icing (confectioners') sugar, to dust (optional)

1 Preheat the oven to 160°C (315°F/Gas 2–3). Lightly grease and flour a deep 18 cm (7 inch) round cake tin, shaking out any excess flour. Beat the butter and sugar with electric beaters until pale and creamy. Add the eggs a little at a time, beating well after each addition. Fold in the flours, lemon zest and milk until combined. When smooth, spoon into the prepared tin and level the surface. Sprinkle with the caster sugar over the top of the surface.

2 Bake for 50 minutes, or until a skewer comes out clean when inserted into the centre of the cake. Allow to cool for 15 minutes in the tin before turning out onto a wire rack to cool completely. If desired, dust with icing sugar.

Gently fold the flour, lemon zest and milk into the egg mixture with a metal spoon.

Evenly sprinkle caster sugar over the top of the mixture before placing in the oven for baking.

Swiss roll

PREPARATION TIME: 25 MINUTES | TOTAL COOKING TIME: 12 MINUTES | SERVES 10

90 g (3¼ oz/¾ cup) self-raising flour
3 eggs, lightly beaten
185 g (6½ oz/¾ cup) caster (superfine) sugar
160 g (5½ oz/½ cup) strawberry jam
    (see HINT)

1 Preheat the oven to 210°C (415°F/Gas 6–7). Lightly grease a 30 x 25 x 2 cm (12 x 10 x ¾ inch) Swiss roll (jelly roll) tin. Line the base with baking paper, extending over the two long sides. Sift the flour three times on a large sheet of baking paper.

2 Using electric beaters, beat the eggs in a mixing bowl until thick and pale. Add 125 g (4½ oz/½ cup) of the sugar gradually, beating constantly until the mixture is pale and glossy.

3 Transfer to a large mixing bowl. Using a metal spoon, fold in the flour quickly and lightly. Spread into the tin and smooth the surface. Bake for 10–12 minutes, or until lightly golden and springy to touch. Meanwhile, place a clean tea towel (dish towel) on a surface, cover with baking paper and lightly sprinkle with the remaining caster sugar. Turn cooked cake out immediately onto the sugar.

4 Using the tea towel as a guide, carefully roll the cake up from the short side, rolling the paper inside the roll. Stand the rolled cake on a wire rack for 5 minutes, then carefully unroll and allow the cake to cool to room temperature. Remove the paper, spread with the jam and re-roll. Trim the ends.

HINT: *Beat the jam with a spatula for 30 seconds before applying to the cake. This makes it easier to spread. Any type of jam can be used.*

Prepare a Swiss roll tin by lining it with baking paper, making sure the paper extends over two sides.

Sift the flour three times so it is well aerated, then quickly fold into the mixture.

Turn the cake out onto baking paper sprinkled with sugar and roll up. Set aside for 5 minutes.

Strawberry mousse sponge

PREPARATION TIME: 35 MINUTES + 2–3 HOURS CHILLING | TOTAL COOKING TIME: 30 MINUTES | SERVES 8

510 g (1 lb 2 oz) packet French vanilla cake
  mix
3 eggs
80 ml (2½ fl oz/⅓ cup) vegetable oil
500 g (1 lb 2 oz) fresh strawberries, hulled
60 g (2¼ oz/¼ cup) caster (superfine) sugar
2 teaspoons powdered gelatine
125 ml (4 fl oz/½ cup) cream
1 egg white

1   Preheat the oven to 180°C (350°F/Gas 4). Lightly grease two round 20 cm (8 inch) shallow cake tins and line each base with baking paper. Using electric beaters, beat the cake mix, eggs, oil and 290 ml (10 fl oz) water on low speed for 30 seconds. Increase to medium speed and continue beating for 2 minutes, or until well combined. Evenly divide the mixture into the prepared tins and bake for 25–30 minutes, or until a skewer comes out clean when inserted into the centre of each cake. Leave in the tins for 5 minutes before turning out onto a wire rack to cool completely.

2   Place 250 g (9 oz) of the strawberries in a food processor and blend until smooth. Stir in the sugar. Pour the strawberry mixture into a saucepan and bring to the boil, then take off the heat. Sprinkle in the gelatine, whisking until dissolved. Transfer to a bowl and set aside to cool. Slice half of the remaining strawberries and set aside the remaining whole strawberries to serve with the cake. Beat the cream until soft peaks form. Using electric beaters, beat the egg white in a clean, dry bowl until soft peaks form. Fold one-third of the cream into the cooled strawberry mixture, then fold in the egg white until combined. Refrigerate for 20 minutes.

3   Trim the top off one of the cakes to level the surface, then place on a serving plate. Fill with three-quarters of the mousse and arrange the sliced strawberries on top. Spread the underside of the other cake with the remaining mousse so it will stick and place it on top. Refrigerate the cake for 2½ hours before serving with the remaining cream.

Divide the cake mixture between two prepared tins and bake for 25–30 minutes.

Fold the beaten egg white into the cooled strawberry mixture then spread on the cake.

Place the sliced strawberries on top of the layer of mousse and top with the other cake.

Hawaiian macadamia cake

PREPARATION TIME: **10** MINUTES | TOTAL COOKING TIME: **1** HOUR | SERVES **10–12**

375 g (13 oz/3 cups) self-raising flour
1 teaspoon ground cinnamon
185 g (6½ oz/1½ cups) caster (superfine) sugar
90 g (3¼ oz/1 cup) desiccated coconut
5 eggs, lightly beaten
440 g (15½ oz) tinned crushed pineapple in syrup
375 ml (13 fl oz/1½ cups) vegetable oil
100 g (3½ oz/¾ cup) chopped macadamia nuts

1 Preheat the oven to 180°C (350°F/Gas 4). Lightly grease a 23 cm (9 inch) round deep cake tin. Line the base and side with two sheets of baking paper, cutting it to make a collar that sits 2–3 cm (¾–1¼ inches) above the side of the tin. Sift the flour and cinnamon into a bowl, add the sugar and coconut and stir to combine. Add the eggs, pineapple and oil and mix well. Stir in the macadamia nuts.

2 Spoon the mixture into the prepared tin and level the surface. Bake for 1 hour, or until a skewer comes out clean when inserted into the centre of the cake. Cover the cake with foil if it is browning too much. Leave in the tin for 30 minutes before turning out onto a wire rack to cool.

STORAGE: *Will keep for 1 week in an airtight container in the fridge.*

Make sure all the ingredients are well combined before folding in the chopped macadamia nuts.

Test to see if the cake is cooked by inserting a skewer in the middle.

Lemon semolina cake

PREPARATION TIME: 25 MINUTES | TOTAL COOKING TIME: 45 MINUTES | SERVES 8–10

6 eggs, separated
310 g (11 oz/1¼ cups) caster (superfine) sugar
2 teaspoons finely grated lemon zest
80 ml (2½ fl oz/⅓ cup) lemon juice
90 g (3¼ oz/¾ cup) semolina
95 g (3¼ oz) ground almonds
2 tablespoons self-raising flour
thick (double/heavy) cream, to serve

1 Preheat the oven to 170°C (325°F/Gas 3). Grease a 24 cm (9½ inch) spring-form cake tin and line with baking paper. Using electric beaters, beat the egg yolks, 250 g (9 oz/1 cup) of the sugar, the zest and 2 tablespoons of the lemon juice in a mixing bowl for 8 minutes, or until thick and pale and the mixture leaves a trail when the beaters are lifted.

2 Beat the egg whites in a clean bowl with electric beaters until firm peaks form. Gently fold the whites with a metal spoon into the egg yolk mixture alternately with the combined semolina, ground almonds and flour. Take care not to overmix. Carefully pour the mixture into the prepared tin and smooth the surface. Bake for 35–40 minutes, or until a skewer comes out clean when inserted into the centre of the cake. Leave the cake in the tin for 5 minutes then turn out onto a wire rack to cool completely. Pierce a few holes in the cake with a skewer.

3 Place the remaining lemon juice and sugar in a saucepan with 125 ml (4 fl oz/½ cup) water. Stir over low heat until the sugar is dissolved. Increase the heat and simmer for 3 minutes, or until thick and syrupy. Pour the hot syrup over the cooled cake. Serve with the cream.

Use a metal spoon to fold the egg whites into the egg yolk mixture with minimal loss of volume.

Simmer the sugar mixture until it is thick and syrupy. Take care as it will be very hot.

Caramel peach cake

PREPARATION TIME: 25 MINUTES + 30 MINUTES STANDING | TOTAL COOKING TIME: 1 HOUR 25 MINUTES | SERVES 8–10

250 g (9 oz) unsalted butter, softened

60 g (2¼ oz/⅓ cup) lightly packed soft brown sugar

1½ x 825 g (1 lb 13 oz) tinned peach halves in natural juice, drained

250 g (9 oz/1 cup) caster (superfine) sugar

3 teaspoons finely grated lemon zest

3 eggs, lightly beaten

385 g (13½ oz/2⅔ cups) self-raising flour, sifted

250 g (9 oz/1 cup) plain yoghurt

1 Preheat the oven to 180°C (350°F/Gas 4). Lightly grease a deep 23 cm (9 inch) round cake tin and line the base with baking paper. Melt 50 g (1¾ oz) of the butter and pour on the base of the tin. Evenly sprinkle the brown sugar on top. Drain the peaches, reserving 1 tablespoon of the liquid. Arrange the peach halves, cut side up, over the sugar mixture.

2 Beat the caster sugar, lemon zest and remaining butter with electric beaters for 5–6 minutes, or until pale and creamy. Add the egg a little at a time, beating well after each addition. The mixture may look curdled but it will come together once the flour is added.

3 Using a metal spoon, fold in the flour alternately with the yoghurt (in two batches) then the reserved peach liquid. Spoon the mixture over the peaches in the tin and smooth the surface. Bake for 1 hour 25 minutes, or until a skewer comes out clean when inserted into the centre of the cake. Leave to cool in the tin for 30 minutes before carefully turning out onto a large serving plate.

Make sure you place the peaches closely together over the sugar mixture.

Use a metal spoon to gently fold the flour and yoghurt into the mixture.

Apple and spice teacake

PREPARATION TIME: 35 MINUTES | TOTAL COOKING TIME: 45–50 MINUTES | SERVES 10

180 g (6 oz) unsalted butter
95 g (3¼ oz/½ cup) lightly packed soft brown
    sugar
2 teaspoons finely grated lemon zest
3 eggs, lightly beaten
250 g (9 oz/1 cup) self-raising flour
75 g (2½ oz/½ cup) wholemeal (whole-wheat)
    flour
½ teaspoon ground cinnamon
250 ml (9 fl oz/1 cup) milk
410 g (14½ oz) tinned pie apples
¼ teaspoon mixed (pumpkin pie) spice
1 tablespoon soft brown sugar, extra
25 g (1 oz/¼ cup) flaked almonds

1 Preheat the oven to 180°C (350°F/Gas 4).
Lightly grease a 20 cm (8 inch) spring-form cake
tin and line the base with baking paper. Using
electric beaters, beat the butter and sugar until
light and creamy. Beat in the lemon zest. Add the
egg gradually, beating well.

2 Fold the sifted flours and cinnamon into
the mixture alternately with the milk. Spoon
half the mixture into the prepared tin, top with
three-quarters of the pie apple then top with the
remaining cake batter. Press the remaining pie
apple around the edge of the top. Combine the
mixed spice, extra sugar and flaked almonds and
sprinkle them over the cake.

3 Bake for 45–50 minutes, or until a skewer
comes out clean when inserted in the centre.
Remove from the tin and allow to cool
completely on a wire rack.

Cream the butter and sugar, then add the lemon
zest followed by the egg.

Spoon the apple onto half the batter then cover with
the remaining batter.

The cake is cooked when a skewer inserted into the
middle comes out clean.

Sour cherry cake

PREPARATION TIME: 20 MINUTES | TOTAL COOKING TIME: 40–45 MINUTES | SERVES 8–10

125 g (4½ oz) unsalted butter, softened
185 g (6½ oz/¾ cup) caster (superfine) sugar
2 eggs, lightly beaten
95 g (3¼ oz) ground almonds
125 g (4½ oz/1 cup) self-raising flour
60 g (2¼ oz/½ cup) plain (all-purpose) flour
125 ml (4 fl oz/½ cup) milk
680 g (1 lb 8 oz) jar pitted morello cherries, well drained
icing (confectioners') sugar, to dust

1   Preheat the oven to 180°C (350°F/Gas 4). Grease and flour a 20 cm (8 inch) fluted baba tin, shaking out any excess flour. Beat the butter and sugar with electric beaters until pale. Add the beaten egg a little at a time, beating well after each addition.

2   Stir in the ground almonds, then fold in the sifted flours alternately with the milk. Gently fold in the cherries. Spoon the mixture into the prepared tin and smooth the surface. Bake for 40–45 minutes, or until a skewer comes out clean when inserted into the centre of the cake. Leave to cool in the tin for 10 minutes before turning out onto a wire rack to cool. Dust with icing sugar before serving.

NOTE: *This cake is best eaten on the day it is made.*

Beat the butter and sugar until the mixture is pale in colour but not creamy.

Gently fold in the cherries, taking care not to break them up with the spoon.

Flourless orange and almond cake

PREPARATION TIME: 15 MINUTES | TOTAL COOKING TIME: 1 HOUR 20 MINUTES | SERVES 8–10

2 small oranges
280 g (10 oz) ground almonds
250 g (9 oz/1 cup) caster (superfine) sugar
1 teaspoon baking powder
1 teaspoon vanilla essence
1 teaspoon Cointreau (orange liquor)
6 eggs, lightly beaten
icing (confectioners') sugar, to dust

1 Wash the oranges to remove any sprays or waxes. Place the whole oranges in a large saucepan, add enough water to cover them and place a small plate on top to keep the oranges submerged. Gradually bring the water to the boil, then reduce the heat and leave to simmer for 40 minutes, or until the oranges are very soft. Preheat the oven to 180°C (350°F/Gas 4). Line the base of a 24 cm (9½ inch) spring-form cake tin with baking paper.

2 Cut each of the oranges into quarters and leave the pieces to cool. Remove any pips, then place the oranges in a food processor and blend until they form a very smooth pulp. Add the ground almonds, sugar, baking powder, vanilla and Cointreau and, using the pulse button, process until combined. Add the egg and process again until just combined—take care not to over-process. Pour the orange mixture into the prepared tin and bake for 40 minutes, or until the cake is firm and leaves the side of the tin. Leave to cool completely in the tin. Dust with icing sugar to serve.

STORAGE: *Will keep for 5 days in a cool place in an airtight container, or for 10 days in the fridge.*

VARIATION: *Try this cake with an orange syrup. Place 500 ml (17 fl oz/2 cups) fresh orange juice in a pan with 185 g (6½ oz/¾ cup) caster (superfine) sugar and 60 ml (2 fl oz/¼ cup) Sauternes. Place the pan over medium heat and stir until the sugar has dissolved. Reduce heat and simmer until liquid is reduced by half and syrupy. Skim any scum off the surface. Drizzle the syrup over the cake and dust with icing sugar.*

The oranges should be quite soft; if a sharp knife cuts into them easily, they are done.

Pour the batter into the prepared tin. It will be quite thick and may look slightly lumpy.

Pistachio, yoghurt and cardamom cake

PREPARATION TIME: 25 MINUTES I TOTAL COOKING TIME: 55 MINUTES I SERVES 8–10

150 g (5½ oz/1 cup) unsalted pistachio nuts
½ teaspoon ground cardamom
150 g (5½ oz) unsalted butter, chopped
185 g (6½ oz/1½ cups) self-raising flour
310 g (10 oz/1¼ cups) caster (superfine) sugar
3 eggs
125 g (4½ oz/½ cup) plain yoghurt
1 lime

1   Preheat the oven to 180°C (350°F/Gas 4). Grease a 20 cm (8 inch) round cake tin and line the base with baking paper. Place the pistachio nuts and cardamom in a food processor and process until just chopped. Add the butter, flour and 185 g (6½ oz/¾ cup) of the caster sugar and process for 20 seconds, or until the mixture is crumbly. Add the combined eggs and yoghurt and process for another 10 seconds, or until everything is just combined.

2   Spoon into the prepared tin and smooth the surface. Bake for 45–50 minutes, or until a skewer comes out clean when inserted into the centre of the cake. Leave the cake in the tin for 5 minutes before turning out onto a wire rack to cool completely.

3   To make the syrup, peel the skin off the lime with a vegetable peeler and make sure the white pith is removed. Place the remaining caster sugar and 100 ml (3½ fl oz) water in a small saucepan and stir over low heat until the sugar has dissolved. Bring to the boil, then add the lime peel and cook for 5 minutes. Strain and cool slightly. Pierce the cake several times with a skewer then pour the hot syrup over.

Process the mixture until it has the texture of fresh breadcrumbs.

Put the mixture into the prepared tin and smooth the surface with a spatula.

Peel the skin off the lime, carefully avoiding the bitter white pith.

Zesty olive oil cake

PREPARATION TIME: 15 MINUTES | TOTAL COOKING TIME: 40 MINUTES | SERVES 8

2 eggs
160 g (5½ oz/⅔ cup) caster (superfine) sugar
2 teaspoons finely grated orange zest
2 teaspoons finely grated lemon zest
125 ml (4 fl oz/½ cup) olive oil
185 g (6½ oz/1½ cups) self-raising flour
60 ml (2 fl oz/¼ cup) milk
60 ml (2 fl oz/¼ cup) orange juice

1 Preheat the oven to 180°C (350°F/Gas 4). Lightly grease a shallow 20 cm (8 inch) round cake tin and line the base with baking paper. Whisk the eggs and sugar in a large mixing bowl until well combined. Add the orange and lemon zest, then gradually stir in the olive oil.

2 Stir in the sifted flour alternately with the milk and orange juice. Stir the mixture gently for 30 seconds with a wooden spoon. Pour into the prepared tin. Bake for 40 minutes, or until a skewer comes out clean when inserted into the centre of the cake. Leave to cool in the tin for 5 minutes before turning out onto a wire rack.

NOTE: *This cake can be dusted with icing (confectioners') sugar before serving, if desired.*

Gradually add the olive oil to the cake mixture, making sure it is well combined.

Gently stir the mixture then pour into the prepared cake tin and bake for 40 minutes.

Coffee syrup cake

PREPARATION TIME: 45 MINUTES I TOTAL COOKING TIME: 45–50 MINUTES I SERVES 8–10

185 g (6½ oz) unsalted butter
185 g (6½ oz/¾ cup) caster (superfine) sugar
3 eggs, separated
1 teaspoon grated lemon zest
250 g (9 oz/1 cup) sour cream
60 g (2¼ oz/¼ cup) plain yoghurt
235 g (8½ oz/1⅔ cups) self-raising flour
25 g (1 oz/¼ cup) ground almonds
whipped cream, to serve
chocolate curls, to serve

SYRUP
250 ml (9 fl oz/1 cup) strong coffee
125 g (4½ oz/½ cup) caster (superfine) sugar
2 tablespoons cognac

1   Preheat the oven to 180°C (350°F/Gas 4). Lightly grease a 23 cm (9 inch) fluted ring tin. Dust the tin with flour, shaking out any excess. Using electric beaters, beat the butter and sugar in a mixing bowl until light and creamy. Add the egg yolks one at time, beating after each addition. Add the zest and beat well. Add the combined sour cream and yoghurt alternately with the sifted flour. Stir in the ground almonds.

2   Using electric beaters, beat the egg whites until stiff peaks form. Using a metal spoon, fold the egg whites into the flour mixture. Spoon into the prepared tin and bake for 5 minutes. Reduce the temperature to 160°C (315°F/ Gas 2–3). Bake for another 40 minutes, or until a skewer comes out clean when inserted into the centre of the cake. Stand the cake in the tin for 5 minutes before turning out onto a wire rack to cool completely.

3   To make the syrup, combine the coffee, sugar and cognac in a saucepan over low heat without boiling until the sugar is dissolved. Bring to the boil, then simmer for 3 minutes to reduce. Remove from the heat and cool slightly.

4   Stand the cake on a wire rack over a baking tray and skewer random holes on top. Spoon the syrup over and collect any excess syrup from the tray to spoon over again. Cool. Serve the cake with whipped cream and chocolate curls.

Beat the butter and sugar together until they become light, creamy and pale in colour.

Spoon the mixture into the prepared tin and smooth the surface.

Skewer random holes on top, then spoon the syrup over several times so it is well soaked.

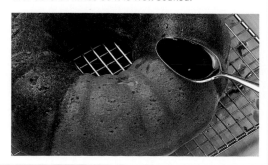

Jam and cream sponge

PREPARATION TIME: 20 MINUTES | TOTAL COOKING TIME: 20 MINUTES | SERVES 8

60 g (2¼ oz/½ cup) plain (all-purpose) flour
60 g (2¼ oz/½ cup) self-raising flour
4 eggs, separated
160 g (5½ oz/⅔ cup) caster (superfine) sugar
4 tablespoons jam
125 ml (4 fl oz/½ cup) whipped cream
icing (confectioners') sugar, to dust

1   Preheat the oven to 180°C (350°F/Gas 4). Grease two shallow 20 cm (8 inch) sandwich tins. Sift the flours three times onto baking paper. Place the egg whites in a large mixing bowl. Using electric beaters, beat the egg whites until stiff peaks form. Add the sugar gradually, beating constantly until the sugar has dissolved and the mixture is thick and glossy.

2   Add the egg yolks and beat for another 20 seconds. Using a metal spoon, fold in the flour quickly and lightly. Spread the mixture evenly into the prepared tins and smooth the surface. Bake for 20 minutes, or until lightly golden and springy to the touch. Leave cakes in the tins for 5 minutes before turning out onto wire racks to cool completely.

3   Spread the jam evenly onto one of the sponges. Spread whipped cream over the jam. Top with the second sponge and dust with sifted icing sugar before serving.

STORAGE: *Unfilled sponges can be frozen for up to a month. Thaw cakes at room temperature for 20 minutes. Serve filled sponges immediately.*

Using electric beaters, beat the egg white and sugar mixture until thick and glossy.

Spread the mixture into tins and smooth the surface with a flat-bladed knife.

Once you have put the sponge together, generously dust with icing sugar.

Coconut syrup cake

PREPARATION TIME: 20 MINUTES + 2 HOURS SOAKING I TOTAL COOKING TIME: 50 MINUTES I SERVES 12

200 g (7 oz) unsalted butter, softened
375 g (13 oz/1½ cups) caster (superfine) sugar
6 eggs
185 g (6½ oz/1½ cups) self-raising flour
270 g (9½ oz/3 cups) desiccated coconut

SYRUP
1 tablespoon lemon zest
375 g (13 oz/1½ cups) sugar

1 Preheat the oven to 180°C (350°F/Gas 4).
Lightly grease and flour a 2 litre (70 fl oz/
8 cup) fluted baba or ring tin, shaking out any
excess flour. Using electric beaters, beat the
butter and sugar for 5 minutes, or until light and
creamy. Add the eggs one at a time, beating well
after each addition, until combined. Fold in the
flour and coconut and mix well.

2 Spoon the mixture into the prepared tin and
bake for 45 minutes, or until a skewer comes out
clean when inserted into the centre of the cake.
Cool slightly in the tin, then turn out onto a wire
rack to cool completely.

3 To make the syrup, place the zest, sugar
and 250 ml (9 fl oz/1 cup) water in a small
saucepan. Stir over medium heat until the sugar
is dissolved. Cool to room temperature. Pierce
the cake all over with a skewer, pour the syrup
over the cake and leave for 2 hours to soak up
the syrup.

Stop beating the butter and sugar together when the mixture looks pale and creamy.

Spoon the cake mixture into the prepared tin, making sure it is evenly distributed.

Pour the cooled syrup over the top of the cake and set aside for 2 hours.

Browned butter and cinnamon teacake

PREPARATION TIME: 30 MINUTES + 15 MINUTES COOLING | TOTAL COOKING TIME: 40 MINUTES | SERVES 9–12

150g (5½ oz) unsalted butter
185 g (6½ oz/1½ cups) self-raising flour
30 g (1 oz/¼ cup) cornflour (cornstarch)
1 teaspoon ground cinnamon
185 g (6½ oz/¾ cup) caster (superfine) sugar
3 eggs, lightly beaten
1 teaspoon vanilla essence
60 ml (2 fl oz/¼ cup) orange juice
60 ml (2 fl oz/¼ cup) milk
extra ground cinnamon, optional, to decorate

BROWNED CINNAMON ICING
80 g (2¾ oz) unsalted butter
80 g (2¾ oz) icing (confectioners') sugar,
    sifted
½ teaspoon ground cinnamon

1 Preheat the oven to 180°C (350°F/Gas 4). Lightly grease a 20 cm (8 inch) square cake tin and line with baking paper. Grease the paper. In a small saucepan, stir the butter over low heat until melted. Continue to heat the butter until it turns golden brown. Skim any fat solids from the surface. Remove from the heat.

2 Sift the flours and cinnamon into a bowl. Add the sugar and stir. Place the eggs, vanilla, juice, milk and browned butter in a separate bowl and stir until well combined. Make a well in the centre of the dry ingredients and pour the egg mixture in. Using electric mixers, beat mixture on low speed until just moistened. Beat on high speed for 5 minutes, or until mixture is free of lumps and increased in volume.

3 Pour the mixture into the prepared tin and smooth the surface. Bake for 40 minutes, or until a skewer comes out clean when inserted into the centre. Remove from the oven and leave the cake in the tin for 10 minutes before turning out onto a wire rack to cool completely.

4 To make the icing (frosting), brown 30 g (1 oz) of the butter as in Step 1. Cool to room temperature. Using electric beaters, beat the remaining butter and icing sugar until light and creamy. Add the cinnamon and browned butter, beating until smooth and fluffy. Spread over the cake with a flat-bladed knife. Sprinkle with extra ground cinnamon, if desired.

STORAGE: *This cake can be stored for up to 4 days in an airtight container or frozen for up to 3 months without icing.*

Once the butter is melted you will need to skim the fat solids off the surface.

Pour the egg mixture into the flour and cinnamon mixture, then combine with electric beaters.

Test to see if the cake is cooked by inserting a skewer into the centre.

Sand cake

PREPARATION TIME: **10** MINUTES | TOTAL COOKING TIME: **40** MINUTES | SERVES **9**

185 g (6½ oz) unsalted butter, softened
2 teaspoons vanilla essence
250 g (9 oz/1 cup) caster (superfine) sugar
3 eggs
185 g (6½ oz/1½ cups) self-raising flour
60 g (2¼ oz/⅓ cup) rice flour
80 ml (2½ fl oz/⅓ cup) milk

1 Preheat the oven to 180°C (350°F/Gas 4). Lightly grease a 23 cm (9 inch) square cake tin and line the base with baking paper.

2 Beat the butter, vanilla, sugar, eggs, flours and milk with electric beaters at low speed until combined, then beat at medium speed for 3 minutes, or until the mixture is thick and creamy.

3 Pour the mixture into the prepared tin and smooth the surface. Bake for 40 minutes, or until a skewer comes out clean when inserted into the centre of the cake. Leave the cake for 10 minutes in the tin then turn out onto a wire rack to cool completely. Cut into squares to serve.

NOTE: *The squares can be decorated with vanilla icing (frosting), if desired.*

Make sure the cake tin is lightly greased with butter or oil before lining with baking paper.

The cake mixture must be thick and creamy before you can stop beating.

Pour the mixture into the prepared tin and smooth the surface with a spoon.

Blueberry shortcake

PREPARATION TIME: 15 MINUTES | TOTAL COOKING TIME: 1 HOUR | SERVES 8–10

100 g (3½ oz) whole hazelnuts
280 g (10 oz/2¼ cups) self-raising flour
1½ teaspoons ground cinnamon
165 g (5¾ oz/¾ cup) raw (demerara) sugar
150 g (5½ oz) unsalted butter, chopped
2 eggs
165 g (5¾ oz) blueberry jam
1 tablespoon raw (demerara) sugar, extra
whipped cream, to serve

1 Preheat the oven to 180°C (350°F/Gas 4). Lightly grease a deep 20 cm (8 inch) round cake tin and line the base with baking paper. Spread the hazelnuts on a baking tray and bake for 5–10 minutes. Place in a clean tea towel (dish towel) and rub together to remove the skins, then roughly chop.

2 Process the flour, cinnamon, sugar, butter and half the hazelnuts in a food processor until finely chopped. Add the eggs and process until combined. Press half the mixture onto the base of the prepared tin, then spread the jam evenly over the mixture.

3 Lightly knead the remaining hazelnuts into the remaining dough, then press evenly over the jam layer. Sprinkle the extra sugar over the top and bake for 50 minutes, or until a skewer comes out clean when inserted into the centre. Leave in the tin for 15 minutes before turning out onto a wire rack to cool completely. Serve with the whipped cream.

Roast the hazelnuts for 5–10 minutes, wrap in a tea towel, then rub together to remove the skins.

Process in a food processor until the mixture resembles fine breadcrumbs.

Sprinkle the extra sugar over the top then bake for 50 minutes.

Orange poppy seed cake

PREPARATION TIME: 25 MINUTES + 15 MINUTES SOAKING I TOTAL COOKING TIME: 50 MINUTES I SERVES 8

50 g (1¾ oz/⅓ cup) poppy seeds
185 ml (6 fl oz/¾ cup) warm milk
250 g (9 oz/1 cup) caster (superfine) sugar
3 eggs
250 g (9 oz/2 cups) self-raising flour
210 g (7½ oz) unsalted butter, softened
1½ tablespoons finely grated orange zest
250 g (9 oz/2 cups) icing (confectioners')
    sugar
3 tablespoons boiling water

1 Preheat the oven to 180°C (350°F/Gas 4). Lightly grease a 23 cm (9 inch) fluted baba tin. Combine the poppy seeds and milk in a mixing bowl and set aside for at least 15 minutes.

2 Place the caster sugar, eggs, sifted flour, 185 g (6½ oz) of the butter and 3 teaspoons of the grated orange zest in a large mixing bowl. Add the poppy seed mixture and beat with electric beaters on low speed until just combined. Increase to medium speed and beat for another 3 minutes, or until the mixture is thick and pale. Pour evenly into the prepared tin. Bake for 50 minutes, or until a skewer comes out clean when inserted into the centre of the cake. Leave in the tin for 5 minutes then turn out onto a wire rack.

3 To make the icing, melt the remaining butter, then place in a bowl with the icing sugar, remaining zest and the boiling water. Mix together to make a soft icing, then spread over the warm cake.

Place the poppy seeds in a mixing bowl then pour over the warm milk and set aside.

Beat the mixture on low speed until combined, then increase to medium speed.

Make the icing by combining the melted butter, icing sugar, orange zest and boiling water.

Banana peanut butter cake

PREPARATION TIME: 10 MINUTES | TOTAL COOKING TIME: 1 HOUR | SERVES 9–12

125 g (4½ oz) unsalted butter
115 g (4 oz/½ cup) firmly packed brown sugar
90 g (3¼ oz/¼ cup) honey
2 large eggs, lightly beaten
90 g (3¼ oz/⅓ cup) crunchy peanut butter
240 g (8½ oz/1 cup) mashed banana
   (see HINT)
300 g (10½ oz/2 cups) wholemeal (whole-
   wheat) self-raising flour

1   Preheat the oven to 180°C (350°F/Gas 4). Lightly grease one 21 x 14 x 7 cm (8¼ x 5½ x 2¾ inch) loaf (bar) tin. Line with greased baking paper. Using electric beaters, beat the butter, sugar and honey in a small mixing bowl until light and creamy. Add the eggs a little at a time, beating thoroughly after each addition. Add the peanut butter and beat until well combined.

2   Transfer the mixture to a large mixing bowl and stir in the banana. Using a metal spoon, fold in the sifted flour including the husks. Stir until the mixture is just combined and almost smooth.

3   Spoon the mixture evenly into the prepared tin and smooth the surface. Bake for 1 hour or until a skewer comes out clean when inserted in the centre of cake. Leave the cake in the tin for 10 minutes, then turn out onto a wire rack to cool completely. Remove the paper. Serve sliced and spread with butter, if desired.

HINT: *Use soft, ripe bananas for this recipe. Mash the bananas with a fork; do not blend or process or they will add too much moisture.*

Once the mixture is smooth, add the peanut butter and beat again.

Add the mashed banana then fold the sifted flour into the mixture with a metal spoon.

Bake for 1 hour and test to see if the cake is cooked by inserting a skewer into the middle.

Gingerbread apricot upside down cake

PREPARATION TIME: 15 MINUTES | TOTAL COOKING TIME: 45 MINUTES | SERVES 6–8

215 g (7½ oz) unsalted butter

1 x 840 g (1 lb 14 oz) tinned apricot halves, drained, reserving 125 ml (4 fl oz/½ cup) of the syrup

95 g (3¼ oz) firmly packed soft brown sugar

185 g (6½ oz/¾ cup) caster (superfine) sugar

2 eggs

185 g (6½ oz/1½ cups) self-raising flour

60 g (2¼ oz) plain (all-purpose) flour

1½ teaspoons ground ginger

½ teaspoon ground nutmeg

1 Preheat the oven to 180°C (350°F/Gas 4). Lightly grease a deep 20 cm (8 inch) round cake tin and line with baking paper. Melt 90 g (3¼ oz) of the butter in a small saucepan over low heat and pour in the tin. Arrange the apricots around the base, cut side up. Scatter the brown sugar over the top.

2 Using electric beaters, cream the remaining butter and caster sugar in a mixing bowl until pale and thick. Add the eggs, one at a time, beating well after each addition.

3 Sift the flours, ginger and nutmeg together and fold into the creamed mixture alternately with the reserved syrup. Spoon the mixture over the apricots. Bake for 45 minutes, or until a skewer comes out clean when inserted into the centre of the cake. Leave in the tin for 15 minutes before turning out onto a wire rack to cool.

STORAGE: *The cake will keep for 4 days in an airtight container.*

Place the apricots around the base of the tin, then sprinkle the brown sugar over the top.

The cake is cooked when a skewer comes out clean when inserted into the centre.

Prune and ricotta cheesecake

PREPARATION TIME: 30 MINUTES | TOTAL COOKING TIME: 2 HOURS | SERVES 8–10

150 g (5½ oz) pitted prunes, chopped
2 tablespoons Marsala
500 g (1 lb 2 oz) dry ricotta cheese
250 g (9 oz/1 cup) caster (superfine) sugar
3 eggs, lightly beaten
125 ml (4 fl oz/½ cup) cream
60 g (2¼ oz/½ cup) cornflour (cornstarch), sifted
60 g (2¼ oz/½ cup) grated chocolate
icing (confectioners') sugar, to dust

1   Preheat the oven to 160°C (315°F/ Gas 2–3). Lightly grease a 23 cm (9 inch) round cake tin and line the base with baking paper. Combine the chopped prunes and Marsala in a small saucepan. Bring to the boil, reduce heat and then simmer for 30 seconds, or until the Marsala is absorbed. Allow to cool.

2   Using electric beaters, beat the ricotta and sugar in a large mixing bowl for 4 minutes, or until light and creamy. Add the egg, a little at a time, beating well after each addition. Add the cream and beat for 2 minutes. Gently fold in the cornflour, prune mixture and chocolate with a metal spoon.

3   Spoon the mixture into the prepared tin and bake for 1¾–2 hours, or until firm and a skewer comes out clean when inserted into the centre. Leave in the tin for 15–20 minutes before gently turning out onto a wire rack to cool. Dust with icing sugar and serve.

Heat the prunes and Marsala together until all the liquid is absorbed.

Place the ricotta and sugar in a mixing bowl, add the egg and cream then beat until light and creamy.

Fold the remaining ingredients into the mixture and place in the prepared cake tin.

Fruit mince and nut cake

PREPARATION TIME: 40 MINUTES + 3 HOURS STANDING | TOTAL COOKING TIME: 2½–3 HOURS | SERVES 10

185 g (6½ oz/1½ cups) plain (all-purpose) flour
60 g (2¼ oz/½ cup) self-raising flour
1 teaspoon mixed (pumpkin pie) spice
140 g (5 oz/¾ cup) lightly packed soft brown sugar
170 g (5¾ oz) raisins
160 g (5½ oz) sultanas (golden raisins)
200 g (7 oz/2 cups) pecans
100 g (3½ oz) mixed raw nuts, chopped
250 g (9 oz) unsalted butter, melted and cooled
425 g (15 oz) ready-made fruit mince (mincemeat)
1 green apple, peeled and grated
2 tablespoons orange marmalade
2 tablespoons rum
2 eggs, lightly beaten

1 Preheat the oven to 160°C (315°F/ Gas 2–3). Lightly grease a 20 cm (8 inch) round cake tin and line the base and side with baking paper. Line the outside of the tin with a double thickness of brown paper and secure with string.

2 Sift the flours and mixed spice into a large bowl. Add the sugar, raisins, sultanas and nuts, reserving half of the pecans. Make a well in the centre of the dry ingredients. Add the butter, fruit mince, grated apple, marmalade, rum and egg and stir until well combined.

3 Spoon the mixture evenly into the prepared tin and smooth the surface. Decorate with the reserved pecans. Bake for 2½–3 hours or until a skewer comes out clean when inserted in the centre of the cake. Allow the cake to cool in the tin overnight before turning out.

Wrap a double layer of brown paper around the cake tin and use string to secure.

Once all the ingredients have been added, stir well to combine.

Try any decorative pattern you like when placing the remaining pecans on top of the cake.

Chocolate cherry cake

PREPARATION TIME: 30 MINUTES | TOTAL COOKING TIME: 1 HOUR 10 MINUTES | SERVES 8

200 g (7 oz) dark chocolate, chopped
250 g (9 oz) unsalted butter, chopped
230 g (8 oz/1 cup) firmly packed soft brown
   sugar
1 teaspoon vanilla essence
155 g (5½ oz/1¼ cups) self-raising flour
45 g (1½ oz/½ cup) desiccated coconut
2 eggs
180 g (6 oz) pitted sour cherries, drained
icing (confectioners') sugar, to dust (optional)
fresh cherries, to garnish (optional)

1 Preheat the oven to 160°C (315°F/Gas 2–3). Lightly grease a 23 cm (9 inch) round cake tin and line the base with baking paper. Grease the paper. Place the chocolate, butter, sugar and vanilla in a heatproof bowl. Sit the bowl, making sure the base does not touch the water, over a saucepan of simmering water. Stir occasionally until the chocolate has melted and the mixture is smooth. Remove the saucepan from the heat and sit the bowl in a sink of cold water until cooled.

2 Combine the flour and coconut in a food processor. Add the chocolate mixture and eggs and process in short bursts until the mixture is just combined. Add the cherries and process until they are just chopped.

3 Pour the mixture into the prepared tin and bake for 1 hour 10 minutes, or until a skewer comes out clean when inserted into the centre of the cake. Leave the cake in the tin for 15 minutes before carefully turning out onto a wire rack to cool completely. If desired, dust with icing sugar and decorate with fresh cherries.

Stir the chocolate, butter, sugar and vanilla in a heatproof bowl.

Add the chocolate mixture and eggs to the food processor with the flour and the coconut.

Leave the cake in the tin before turning out onto a wire rack to cool.

Marbled blueberry cake

PREPARATION TIME: 30 MINUTES I TOTAL COOKING TIME: 50–55 MINUTES I SERVES 8

1 tablespoon sugar
195 g (6¾ oz/1¼ cups) fresh blueberries,
   plus extra, to serve (see VARIATION)
2 eggs
½ teaspoon vanilla essence
125 g (4½ oz) unsalted butter
165 g (5¾ oz/1⅓ cups) self-raising flour, sifted
125 g (4½ oz/½ cup) caster (superfine) sugar
2 tablespoons soft brown sugar
icing (confectioners') sugar, to dust
whipped cream, to serve

1   Preheat the oven to 180°C (350°F/Gas 4). Lightly grease a 20 cm (8 inch) round spring-form cake tin and line the base and side with baking paper. Place the sugar and half the blueberries in a small saucepan. Stir together gently over medium heat for 1–2 minutes or until the juices begin to run. Remove from the heat. Stir in the remaining blueberries, then allow the mixture to cool.

2   Beat the eggs in a small mixing bowl. Add the vanilla and butter and mix well. Combine the flour and caster sugar in a separate mixing bowl. Make a well in the centre. Using a metal spoon, stir in the egg mixture until smooth.

3   Take out ¾ cup of the cake mixture and stir into the blueberries. Place spoonfuls of both mixtures randomly into the prepared tin. Swirl the mixture with a knife or skewer to produce a marbled effect. Do not overmix the blueberries and cake mixture or they will blend, rather than looking nicely swirled. Sprinkle the brown sugar over the top. Bake for 45–50 minutes, or until a skewer comes out clean when inserted into the centre. Stand the cake in its tin on a wire rack to cool for 5 minutes before removing and allowing it to cool completely. Serve the cake dusted liberally with icing sugar, or decorate with extra berries and cream.

STORAGE: *This cake is best eaten on the day it is made.*

VARIATION: *Raspberries can also be used in this cake if blueberries are out of season.*

Stir the blueberries over medium heat until they start to release their juices.

Use a metal spoon to fold the egg mixture into the dry ingredients.

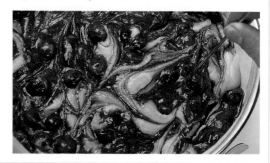
Carefully swirl the different coloured mixtures together, making sure not to overmix them.

Rum and raisin cake

PREPARATION TIME: 15 MINUTES + 10 MINUTES SOAKING | TOTAL COOKING TIME: 45 MINUTES | SERVES 8

160 g (5½ oz) raisins
60 ml (2 fl oz/¼ cup) dark rum
185 g (6½ oz/1½ cups) self-raising flour
60 g (2¼ oz/½ cup) plain (all-purpose) flour
150 g (5½ oz) unsalted butter, chopped
140 g (5 oz/¾ cup) lightly packed soft brown sugar
3 eggs, lightly beaten
ice cream, to serve

1 Preheat the oven to 180°C (350°F/Gas 4). Lightly grease a deep 20 cm (8 inch) round cake tin and line the base with baking paper. Soak the raisins and rum in a small bowl for 10 minutes. Sift the flours into a large mixing bowl and make a well in the centre.

2 Melt the butter and sugar in a small saucepan over low heat, stirring until the sugar is dissolved. Remove from the heat. Combine with the rum and raisin mixture and add to the flour with the egg. Stir, making sure not to overbeat, with a wooden spoon until just combined.

3 Spoon the mixture into the prepared tin and smooth the surface. Bake for 40 minutes, or until a skewer comes out clean when inserted into the centre of the cake. Serve with ice cream.

Place the raisins in a small bowl and pour the rum over. Leave to soak for 10 minutes.

Using a wooden spoon, stir the mixture until all the ingredients are just combined.

The cake is cooked if a skewer inserted into the centre comes out clean.

Chocolate ginger and fig cake

PREPARATION TIME: 15 MINUTES | TOTAL COOKING TIME: 1 HOUR | SERVES 8–10

125 g (4½ oz) unsalted butter, softened
230 g (8 oz/1 cup) firmly packed soft brown
    sugar
2 eggs, lightly beaten
185 g (6½ oz/1½ cups) self-raising flour
40 g (1½ oz/⅓ cup) unsweetened cocoa powder
185 ml (6 fl oz/¾ cup) milk
125 g (4½ oz/⅔ cup) dried figs, chopped
75 g (2½ oz/⅓ cup) glacé (candied) ginger,
    chopped

1 Preheat the oven to 180°C (350°F/Gas 4).
Lightly grease a 22 x 12 cm (8½ x 4½ inch) loaf
(bar) tin and line the base with baking paper.
Using electric beaters, beat the butter and sugar
in a mixing bowl until pale and creamy.

2 Add the egg, a little at a time, beating well
after each addition. Stir in the sifted flour and
cocoa alternately with the milk to make a smooth
batter. Fold in the figs and half the ginger.

3 Spoon the mixture into the prepared tin and
smooth the surface. Scatter the remaining ginger
over the top. Bake for 1 hour, or until a skewer
comes out clean when inserted into the centre of
the cake. Leave to cool in the tin for 5 minutes
before turning out onto a wire rack to cool.

Gently fold the chopped figs and half the ginger
into the mixture with a metal spoon.

Scatter the remaining chopped ginger over the top
after you have smoothed the surface of the mixture.

Apricot pine nut cake

PREPARATION TIME: 25 MINUTES | TOTAL COOKING TIME: 1 HOUR | SERVES 10

100 g (3½ oz/⅔ cup) pine nuts, roughly chopped
250 g (9 oz) unsalted butter, softened
250 g (9 oz/1 cup) sugar
3 teaspoons finely grated orange zest
3 eggs, lightly beaten
310 g (11 oz/2½ cups) self-raising flour, sifted
200 g (7 oz) glacé (candied) apricots, finely chopped (see NOTE)
250 ml (9 fl oz/1 cup) orange juice
icing (confectioners') sugar, to dust (optional)
whipping cream or plain yoghurt, to serve (optional)

1 Preheat the oven to 180°C (350°F/Gas 4). Lightly grease a 26 cm (10½ inch) round cake tin and line the base with baking paper. Spread the pine nuts on a baking tray and bake for 5–10 minutes, or until lightly golden. Set aside to cool.

2 Beat the butter, sugar and orange zest with electric beaters until pale and creamy. Add the eggs a little at a time, beating well after each addition. (The mixture may look curdled but once you add the flour, it will bring it back together.) Fold in the flour, pine nuts, apricots and orange juice in two batches.

3 Spoon the mixture into the prepared tin and smooth the surface. Bake for 50 minutes, or until a skewer comes out clean when inserted into the centre of the cake. Leave the cake in the tin for 10 minutes before turning out onto a wire rack to cool completely. If desired, dust with the icing sugar and serve with whipped cream or yoghurt.

STORAGE: *Will keep for 5 days in a cool place in an airtight container.*

NOTE: *The chopped apricots may clump together, so flour your hands and rub through the apricot to separate the pieces.*

VARIATION: *For a little extra flavour, add 2 tablespoons brandy to the cake mixture with the flour, pine nuts, apricots and orange juice.*

Bake the pine nuts for 5–10 minutes, or until lightly golden brown.

Don't worry if the mixture looks curdled. Once the flour is added, it will come together.

Spoon the mixture into the prepared tin and bake for 50 minutes.

Walnut cake with chocolate icing

PREPARATION TIME: 25 MINUTES | TOTAL COOKING TIME: 40 MINUTES | SERVES 6

185 g (6½ oz) unsalted butter
95 g (3¼ oz/½ cup) lightly packed soft brown
　　sugar
2 eggs
185 g (6½ oz/1½ cups) self-raising flour
60 g (2¼ oz/½ cup) chopped walnuts, plus
　　30 g (1 oz/¼ cup) for decoration
80 ml (2½ fl oz/⅓ cup) milk

CHOCOLATE ICING

20 g (¾ oz) unsalted butter
125 g (4½ oz) good-quality dark chocolate,
　　chopped

1　Preheat the oven to 180°C (350°F/Gas 4). Lightly grease a 20 cm (8 inch) spring-form cake tin and line the base with baking paper. Using electric beaters, beat the butter and sugar in a large mixing bowl for 5 minutes, or until thick and creamy. Add the eggs one at a time, beating well after each addition. Using a metal spoon, fold in the sifted flour and 60 g (2¼ oz/½ cup) of the walnuts alternately with the milk until just combined. Spoon the mixture into the prepared tin and smooth the surface. Bake for 35 minutes, or until a skewer comes out clean when inserted into the centre. Remove from the oven and leave the cake in the tin for 5 minutes before turning out onto a wire rack to cool completely.

2　To make the icing (frosting), place the butter and chocolate in a heatproof bowl. Bring a saucepan of water to the boil, then reduce the heat to a gentle simmer. Sit the bowl over the saucepan, making sure the base of the bowl does not touch the water. Stir occasionally until melted and smooth. Remove from the heat and leave to cool slightly. Spread the icing over the cake with a flat-bladed knife. Sprinkle with the remaining walnuts.

STORAGE: *Will keep in an airtight container for up to 3 days.*

Spoon the mixture into the prepared tin and then smooth the surface with a metal spoon.

Melt the butter and chocolate in a heatproof bowl over a saucepan of simmering water.

Honey and coconut cake

PREPARATION TIME: 40 MINUTES I TOTAL COOKING TIME: 30–35 MINUTES I SERVES 16

125 g (4½ oz) unsalted butter, softened
140 g (5 oz/⅔ cup) raw (demerara) sugar
2 large eggs, lightly beaten
1 teaspoon vanilla essence
90 g (3¼ oz/¼ cup) honey
45 g (1½ oz/½ cup) desiccated coconut
220 g (7¾ oz/1¾ cups) self-raising flour
1 teaspoon ground nutmeg
¼ teaspoon ground cinnamon
¼ teaspoon ground allspice
125 ml (4 fl oz/½ cup) milk

HONEY AND CREAM CHEESE ICING
125 g (4½ oz) cream cheese, softened
60 g (2¼ oz/½ cup) icing (confectioners') sugar
1 tablespoon honey

1   Preheat the oven to 180°C (350°F/Gas 4).
Lightly grease a 28 x 18 x 3 cm (11¼ x 7 x
1¼ inch) cake tin. Line with lightly greased
baking paper. Using electric beaters, beat the
butter and sugar in a small mixing bowl until
light and creamy. Add the eggs, a little at a time,
beating thoroughly after each addition. Add the
vanilla and honey. Beat until well combined.

2   Transfer the mixture to a large mixing
bowl and add the desiccated coconut. Using a
metal spoon, fold in the sifted flour and spices
alternating with the milk. Stir until just combined
and the mixture is almost smooth. Spoon into the
prepared tin and smooth the surface.

3   Bake for 30–35 minutes, or until a skewer
comes out clean when inserted in the centre.
Leave the cake in the tin for 10 minutes before
turning out onto a wire rack to cool. Remove the
baking paper. To make the icing (frosting), beat
the cream cheese with electric beaters in a small
mixing bowl until creamy. Add the sifted icing
sugar and the honey, beating until the mixture is
smooth and fluffy. Spread evenly over the cake
using a flat-bladed knife.

STORAGE: *The cake can be stored for up to*
4 days in an airtight container.

Alternate folding in the milk with the sifted flour
and spices.

Test to see if the cake is cooked by inserting a
skewer into the centre.

Rich dark chocolate cake

PREPARATION TIME: 35 MINUTES | TOTAL COOKING TIME: 1 HOUR 40 MINUTES | SERVES 10–12

185 g (6½ oz) unsalted butter, chopped

250 g (9 oz) dark chocolate chips

220 g (7¾ oz/1¾ cups) self-raising flour

40 g (1½ oz/⅓ cup) unsweetened cocoa
   powder

375 g (13 oz/1½ cups) caster (superfine)
   sugar

3 eggs, lightly beaten

CHOCOLATE TOPPING

20 g (¾ oz) unsalted butter, chopped

125 g (4½ oz) dark chocolate, chopped

1 Preheat the oven to 160°C (315°F/
Gas 2–3). Lightly grease a 22 cm (8½ inch)
spring-form cake tin and line the base with
baking paper. Place the butter and chocolate
chips in a small heatproof bowl. Place the bowl
over a saucepan of simmering water, making
sure the base does not touch the water, and
stir frequently until melted.

2 Sift the flour and cocoa into a large mixing
bowl. Combine the chocolate mixture, sugar
and egg, then add 250 ml (9 fl oz/1 cup) of
water and mix well. Add to the flour and
cocoa and stir until well combined. Pour the
mixture into the prepared tin and bake for 1
hour 30 minutes, or until a skewer comes out
clean when inserted into the centre of the cake.
Leave the cake in the tin for 15 minutes before
turning out onto a wire rack to cool completely.

3 To make the topping, place the butter and
chocolate in a small heatproof bowl. Place
the bowl over a saucepan of simmering water,
making sure the base does not touch the water.
Spread over the cooled cake in a swirl pattern.

Melt the butter and chocolate in a heatproof bowl over a pan of simmering water.

Pour the mixture into the prepared tin and bake for 1 hour 30 minutes.

Using a flat-bladed knife, spread the chocolate topping over the cooled cake.

Date and walnut loaf

PREPARATION TIME: 25 MINUTES | TOTAL COOKING TIME: 1 HOUR | SERVES 9–12

125 g (4½ oz) unsalted butter
350 g (12 oz/½ cup) honey (see HINT)
55 g (2 oz/¼ cup) firmly packed light brown sugar
2 tablespoons milk
280 g (10 oz/1½ cups) chopped stoned dates
¼ teaspoon bicarbonate of soda (baking soda)
250 g (9 oz/2 cups) plain (all-purpose) flour
½ teaspoon ground nutmeg
125 g (4½ oz/1 cup) chopped walnuts
2 eggs, lightly beaten

1 Preheat the oven to 180°C (350°F/Gas 4). Lightly grease one 21 x 14 x 8 cm (8¼ x 5½ x 3¼ inch) loaf (bar) tin and line with baking paper. Grease the baking paper.

2 Combine the butter, honey, brown sugar and milk in a medium saucepan. Stir over low heat until the butter has melted and the sugar has dissolved. Remove from the heat. Stir in the dates and bicarbonate of soda, then set aside to cool. Sift the flour and nutmeg into a large mixing bowl. Add the chopped walnuts and stir. Make a well in the centre of the dry ingredients.

3 Pour the butter mixture and the eggs into the dry ingredients. Using a wooden spoon, stir until well combined but do not overbeat. Spoon evenly into the prepared tin and smooth the surface. Bake for 55 minutes, or until a skewer inserted in the centre of the cake comes out clean. Leave the cake in the tin for 15 minutes, then turn out onto a wire rack. Remove the baking paper. Serve the loaf with extra butter, if desired.

STORAGE: *Store the cake for up to 3 days in an airtight container.*

HINT: *Cakes that are made with honey will stay moist for longer than those made with sugar.*

Constantly stir over a low heat until the butter has melted and the sugar has dissolved.

Pour the butter mixture and the eggs into the well then stir until combined with a wooden spoon.

Custard butter cake

PREPARATION TIME: 30 MINUTES | TOTAL COOKING TIME: 40 MINUTES | SERVES 8–10

250 g (9 oz/2 cups) self-raising flour
110 g (3¾ oz) custard powder
½ teaspoon bicarbonate of soda (baking soda)
185 g (6½ oz) unsalted butter, chopped
275 g (9¾ oz) caster (superfine) sugar
4 eggs, lightly beaten
1 teaspoon vanilla essence
90 ml (3 fl oz) buttermilk

ICING
100 g (3½ oz) white chocolate
60 ml (2 fl oz/¼ cup) cream
200 g (7 oz) cream cheese, softened
40 g (1½ oz/⅓ cup) icing (confectioners') sugar
silver cachous and crystallised violets, to
    decorate

1 Preheat the oven to 180°C (350°F/Gas 4). Lightly grease a deep 20 cm (8 inch) square cake tin and line the base with baking paper. Sift the flour, custard powder and bicarbonate of soda into a bowl and make a well in the centre.

2 Melt the butter and sugar in a heavy-based saucepan over low heat, stirring until the sugar is dissolved. Remove from the heat. Add the butter mixture and combined egg, vanilla and buttermilk to the dry ingredients and stir until just combined. Spoon into the prepared tin. Bake for 35 minutes, or until a skewer comes out clean when inserted into the centre. Leave in the tin to cool.

3 To make the icing, melt the chocolate and cream in a saucepan over low heat. Cool and add to the cream cheese and icing sugar. Beat until smooth. Spread the cake with icing and decorate with silver cachous and crystallised violets.

Sift the dry ingredients into a large mixing bowl and make a well in the centre.

Spoon the mixture into the prepared tin and bake for 35 minutes.

Honey, nut and fruit loaf

PREPARATION TIME: 20 MINUTES | TOTAL COOKING TIME: 1 HOUR 5 MINUTES | SERVES 10

350 g (12 oz/1 cup) honey
45 g (1½ oz) unsalted butter
1 egg
310 g (11 oz/2½ cups) self-raising flour
½ teaspoon bicarbonate of soda (baking soda)
½ teaspoon ground cinnamon
185 ml (6 fl oz/¾ cup) milk
80 g (2¾ oz) chopped pecans
40 g (1½ oz/¼ cup) chopped almonds
60 g (2¼ oz) chopped pitted prunes
45 g (1½ oz/¼ cup) chopped dried apricots
30 g (1 oz/¼ cup) raisins

1   Preheat the oven to 180°C (350°F/Gas 4). Grease a 23 x 15 cm (9 x 6 inch) loaf (bar) tin and line the base with baking paper. Using electric beaters, beat the honey and butter until well combined. Add the egg and beat well. Transfer the mixture to a large mixing bowl.

2   Fold the sifted flour, bicarbonate of soda and cinnamon into the creamed mixture alternately with the milk. Fold in the nuts and fruit.

3   Spoon the cake mixture into the prepared tin and smooth the surface. Bake for 45 minutes, then cover the cake with foil and bake for another 20 minutes, or until a skewer comes out clean when inserted in the centre of the cake. Let the cake cool in the tin for 10 minutes before turning out onto a wire rack to cool completely before serving.

STORAGE: *This cake will keep in an airtight container for up to 3 days.*

To line the loaf tin, trace around the base on baking paper, cut out and fit the paper into the tin.

Lightly fold the chopped nuts and fruit into the mixture with a large metal spoon.

Spoon the mixture into the prepared tin and smooth the surface.

Basics

Cake tins and linings

Cakes can be an easy way to impress, but don't let your masterpiece be spoiled at the last minute as you turn it out of the tin. Follow these simple instructions for perfect results every time.

Cake tins are greased and lined to prevent the mixture from sticking to the tin. Always prepare the tin according to the instructions before preparing the cake.

Check the size of your cake tin by measuring the diameter or width and length of the base. It is important to use the tin size specified in the recipe or at least one of the same cup capacity—check by measuring with water. Aluminium tins give consistently good results. Avoid using dark-coloured tins as they may brown the cake before it cooks through.

Remember—when you start to make your cake, it is very important to read through the recipe first to be sure you have all the necessary ingredients and equipment. Preheat the oven and put the cake on the middle shelf once it has reached the correct temperature.

Greasing and lining the cake tin

Grease the tin using melted unsalted butter or a mild-flavoured oil. Apply just enough to evenly coat the base and sides of the tin using a pastry brush, making sure there is no excess dripping back to the base of the tin—oil sprays are a quick and easy alternative (spray away from the heat source in a well-ventilated area).

Baking paper is the preferred paper for lining cake tins.

Lining the tin

Average-sized cakes generally only need the tin base to be lined, after a light greasing with either melted butter or oil (don't use a strong-flavoured oil), or a light coat of vegetable oil spray. This is because they don't have a particularly long cooking time. Simply place the tin on top of a piece of baking paper, draw around it and cut out the traced shape to fit the base of the tin. Other cakes, such as fruit cake, which are cooked for a much longer time or those with a high sugar content, require extra protection, both around the side and under the base. Generally, with these cakes the oven temperature will be quite low so the best way to do it will be to tie a few layers of newspaper in a cuff around the outside of the tin, and to sit the tin on a wad of newspaper in the oven in addition to greasing and lining it as described before. Because the oven temperature stays low, this is quite safe. When lining the inside of the tins, use a good-quality baking paper, making sure that it is free of any wrinkles that could spoil your cake's smooth finish.

Making a collar (below)

Some of the cakes in this book are cooked with a collar. This extends the height of the cake, giving a more dramatic result. Collars can also give extra protection during cooking.

As a general rule a single layer of baking paper is enough for a collar on an average-sized cake.

Fold down a cuff in one edge of the collar, then make diagonal cuts at intervals up to the fold.

Place the collar around the edge of the tin, pressing the cuts onto the base of the tin.

Fold down a cuff on one edge of the baking paper and cut the cuff up to the fold line.

Place the baking paper along the greased side of the tin, with the cut cuff sitting on the base.

Cut a circle of baking paper to fit into the base of the tin and put it in place.

Larger cakes and fruit cakes will need a double layer of baking paper to make the collar and line the base.

To make a collar, lightly grease the cake tin. Cut a strip of paper long enough to fit around the outside of the tin and tall enough to extend 5 cm (2 inches) above the top of the tin. Fold down one cuff, about 2 cm (¾ inch) deep, along the length of the strip.

Make diagonal cuts up to the fold line about 1 cm (½ inch) apart. Fit the collar around the inside edge of the tin, with the cuts in the base of the tin, pressing them out at right angles so they sit flat around the bottom edge of the tin. Cut a circle of baking paper using the bottom of the tin as a guide. Place the circle of paper in the base of the tin, over the cuts in the collar. Make sure that the paper is smooth and crease-free before pouring in your cake batter or the base and side of your cake will come out with the creases baked into them.

Lining a round cake tin (above)

Step 1: To line the side of a round tin, cut a strip of baking paper long enough to cover the outside of the tin and up to 6 cm (2½ inches) wider than the height. Fold down a 2 cm

(¾ inch) cuff, then cut the cuff on the diagonal at 2 cm (¾ inch) intervals.

Step 2: Grease the inside of the tin and place the strip of baking paper against the inside with the cut cuff sitting neatly on the base— the cut cuff will act like pleats, ensuring that the paper sits snug against the side of the pan.

Step 3: Place the cake tin on a sheet of baking paper and trace around the outside, then cut out with a pair of scissors. Place, pencil-side down, onto the base of the tin over the pleats and smooth out any bubbles. If just lining the base, complete Step 3 only.

Lining a square cake tin (below)

Step 1: Place the cake tin on a sheet of baking paper and trace around the outside with a pencil.

Step 2: Cut out the paper and place, pencil-side down, onto the base of the tin, smoothing out any air bubbles.

Step 3: If lining the sides of the tin as well, cut a strip of baking paper the same length as the outside of the tin and 1 cm (½ inch) wider than the height. Place against the inside around the sides, smoothing out any bubbles.

Use the base of the cake tin to accurately trace the shape onto the baking paper.

Grease the tin, then fit the paper into the base, eliminating any air bubbles as you go.

Cut a strip of baking paper to fit the sides of the tin and smooth them into place.

Cake toppings

Your favourite carrot cake just isn't the same without that delicious cream cheese icing, chocolate cake loses a little of its allure without its rich chocolate topping and a simple butter cake gains five-star standing when partnered with coffee buttercream. The icing (frosting) on the cake can make all the difference.

Ginger and lemon glacé icing

Sift 40 g (1½ oz/⅓ cup) icing (confectioners') sugar into a small heatproof bowl. Add ½ teaspoon ginger, 20 g (¾ oz) melted unsalted butter, 2 teaspoons milk and 1 teaspoon lemon juice and mix to form a paste. Place the bowl over a saucepan of simmering water, making sure the base does not touch the water, and stir until the icing is smooth and glossy. Remove the bowl from the heat. Spread with a knife dipped in hot water for even covering. Do not reheat.

Lemon cream cheese icing

Place 60 g (2¼ oz/¼ cup) softened cream cheese and 30 g (1 oz) unsalted butter in a small mixing bowl. Using electric beaters, beat until combined. Add 1 tablespoon lemon juice and 185 g (6 oz/ 1½ cups) sifted icing (confectioners') sugar and beat until smooth.

Butterscotch frosting

Chop 20 g (¾ oz) unsalted butter into small pieces and place in a saucepan with 95 g (3¼ oz/ ½ cup) lightly packed brown sugar. Stir constantly over low heat until the mixture boils and the sugar dissolves. Simmer for 3 minutes. Remove from the heat, add 90 g (3¼ oz/⅓ cup) sour cream and stir. Leave to cool. Place 100 g (3½ oz) softened cream cheese in a mixing bowl and beat with electric beaters until light and creamy. Add the cooled butterscotch mixture, a little at a time, beating well after each addition.

Chocolate ganache

Combine 60 ml (2 fl oz/¼ cup) cream and 150 g (5½ oz) dark chocolate in a small saucepan. Stir over low heat until the chocolate has melted and the mixture is smooth. Remove from the heat and allow to cool. Pour the ganache on to the cake, then smooth the top and around the side with a flat-bladed knife.

Caramel icing

Place 185 g (6½ oz/¾ cup) icing (confectioners') sugar, 1 tablespoon milk, 2 tablespoons golden syrup and 30 g (1 oz) softened unsalted butter in a bowl and beat with a wooden spoon until smooth.

Coffee buttercream

Dissolve 3 teaspoons instant coffee in 2 tablespoons boiling water. Place 125 g (4½ oz) unsalted butter and 185 g (6½ oz/¾ cup) icing (confectioners') sugar in a mixing bowl. Using electric beaters, beat until pale and creamy. Add ½ teaspoon vanilla essence, the coffee mixture and 2 teaspoons milk and beat for 2 minutes, or until smooth and fluffy.

Lime icing

Place 250 g (9 oz/1 cup) sifted icing (confectioners') sugar, 80 g (2¾ oz) softened unsalted butter and 2 tablespoons lime juice in a mixing bowl and beat with a wooden spoon until smooth, adding 1–2 tablespoons water, if necessary.

Chocolate fudge icing

Coarsely chop 150 g (5½ oz) dark chocolate and place in a small saucepan with 90 g (3¼ oz) unsalted butter and 160 g (5½ oz/ ½ cup) condensed milk. Stir over low heat until the chocolate and butter have melted and the mixture is smooth. Remove from the heat. Allow to cool until thick and spreadable.

Orange glacé icing

Sift 125 g (4½ oz/½ cup) icing (confectioners') sugar into a heatproof bowl. Add 10 g (¼ oz) softened unsalted butter, 1 teaspoon grated orange zest and enough orange juice to make a soft pouring consistency. Place the bowl, making sure the base does not touch the water, over a saucepan of simmering water and stir until the icing is smooth and glossy. Remove from the heat. Drizzle over the cake.

Biscuit icings and toppings

These delicious toppings will add a special touch to even a basic biscuit. Along with the simple recipe provided, even young cooks can produce a masterpiece—with a bit of help from Mum and Dad!

Basic biscuit recipe

Preheat the oven to 160°C (315°F/Gas 2–3). Line a baking tray with baking paper. Using electric beaters, beat together 125 g (4½ oz) cubed unsalted butter and 125 g (4½ oz/½ cup) caster (superfine) sugar until light and fluffy. Add 1 egg and ¼ teaspoon vanilla essence and beat well. Sift 125 g (4½ oz/1 cup) plain (all-purpose) flour and 125 g (4½ oz/1 cup) self-raising flour and fold in to form a soft dough. Turn out onto a sheet of baking paper, cover with another sheet and roll out to 5 mm (¼ inch) thick. Using cookie cutters, cut out shapes and place on the tray. Bake in batches for 10–15 minutes, or until lightly golden. Cool on a wire rack, then spread with your choice of topping (see below and right). Makes about 50 biscuits.

Maple syrup icing

Mix 125 g (4½ oz/½ cup) sifted icing (confectioners') sugar, 2 tablespoons maple syrup and 1 tablespoon softened unsalted butter in a small, heatproof bowl. Stir the mixture over a saucepan of simmering water until the mixture softens and is smooth and easy to spread.

Passionfruit glace icing

Mix 2 tablespoons fresh passionfruit pulp and 155 g (5½ oz) sifted icing (confectioners') sugar in a small, heatproof bowl. Stir the mixture over a saucepan of simmering water until it becomes smooth and glossy. You can use tinned pulp if fresh passionfruit is not in season.

Coconut ice topping

Mix 155 g (5½ oz/1¼ cups) sifted icing (confectioners') sugar, 1 tablespoon softened unsalted butter, 45 g (1½ oz/½ cup) desiccated coconut, ½ teaspoon vanilla essence and a few drops pink food colouring in a bowl. Add 6–8 teaspoons boiling water to make a thick, spreadable mixture.

Vanilla icing

Sift 155 g (5½ oz/1¼ cups) icing (confectioners') sugar into a small bowl. Add 1 tablespoon cubed and softened unsalted butter, ½ teaspoon vanilla essence and 1–2 tablespoons boiling water. Stir until the mixture is smooth and spreadable.

Citrus fruit icing

Put 2 teaspoons each of finely shredded lime zest, lemon zest and orange zest, 60 g (2¼ oz/ ½ cup) sifted icing (confectioners') sugar and 60 ml (2 fl oz/¼ cup) water in a saucepan. Stir constantly over low heat until the sugar dissolves. Simmer, without stirring, for 5 minutes. Remove the zest and drain on a wire rack. Mix together 155 g (5½ oz/1¼ cups) sifted icing (confectioners') sugar, 1 tablespoon softened butter, 2 teaspoons lemon juice, 3 teaspoons lime juice, 2 teaspoons orange juice and the drained zests in a bowl until spreadable.

Choc and nut topping

Sift 155 g (5½ oz/1¼ cups) icing (confectioners') sugar and 1 tablespoon cocoa powder into a bowl. Add 1 tablespoon softened unsalted butter, 1–2 tablespoons boiling water and mix together until smooth. Spread the biscuits with the topping, then sprinkle with chopped, roasted hazelnuts or almonds. The nuts can be replaced by coloured sprinkles for a more colourful effect.

Marshmallow topping

Mix 125 g (4½ oz/½ cup) sifted icing (confectioners') sugar, 1 tablespoon softened unsalted butter and 1 tablespoon boiling water in a bowl until smooth. Add 25 g (1 oz/½ cup) mini marshmallows. Stir over a saucepan of simmering water for 1 minute, or until the marshmallows have just melted. Spread quickly onto the biscuits.

Chocolate fleck icing

Sift 155 g (5½ oz/1¼ cups) icing (confectioners') sugar into a bowl. Add 1 tablespoon softened unsalted butter, ½ teaspoon vanilla essence and 5 teaspoons boiling water. Stir until smooth. Gently mix in 2 tablespoons grated dark chocolate, then spread on the biscuits.

Index

Index

Published in 2009 by Murdoch Books Pty Limited.

Murdoch Books Australia
83 Alexander Street
Crows Nest NSW 2065
Phone: + 61 (0) 8425 0100
Fax: + 61 (0) 9906 2218
www.murdochbooks.com.au

Project manager: Kristin Buesing
Editor: Monica Berton
Design concept: Heather Menzies
Design: Heather Menzies and Jacqueline Richards
Photographer: Valerie Martin
Stylist: Mary Harris
Food preparation: Jo Glynn
Introduction text: Leanne Kitchen
Production: Kita George

National Library of Australia Cataloguing-in-Publication Data
Home Style Cookies, muffins and cakes. Includes index.
ISBN 9781741962727 (pbk.)
Subjects: Cookies. Muffins. Cake.
Dewey Number:
641.865

Colour separation by Splitting Image in Clayton, Victoria, Australia.
Printed by 1010 Printing International Limited, China.
PRINTED IN CHINA. Reprinted 2009, 2010, 2011, 2013.

IMPORTANT: Those who might be at risk from the effects of salmonella poisoning
(the elderly, pregnant women, young children and those suffering from immune deficiency diseases)
should consult their doctor with any concerns about eating raw eggs.

CONVERSION GUIDE: You may find cooking times vary depending on the oven
you are using. For fan-forced ovens, as a general rule, set the oven temperature
to 20°C (35°F) lower than indicated in the recipe.